THE Hull City SAGA

Hull City THE SAGA

The seesaw tale of the Tigers

by David Bond

The Breedon Books
Publishing Company
Derby

First published in Great Britain by
The Breedon Books Publishing Company Limited
Breedon House, 44 Friar Gate, Derby, DE1 1DA.
1999

ISBN 1 85983 1548 6

Printed and bound by
Butler & Tanner Ltd., Selwood Printing Works,
Caxton Road, Frome, Somerset.

Colour separations and jacket printing by
Green Shires Group Ltd, Leicester.

Contents

Chapter One

Then and Now

HULL City AFC have repeatedly been labelled as sleeping giants over the years. They have always been a big-city club, but they have never quite fulfilled their potential as such. At times support for them has been all that might be expected of a club with a large population in their midst: at other times it has dwindled in a morass of anti-climax and despondency. There has long been a high degree of expectancy in the city and its hinterland, but City have infuriatingly and frustratingly managed to flatter to deceive. The term "sleeping giants," accordingly, just becomes a convenient euphemism for "under-achievers."

Fans who have stayed loyal to the Tigers, as they have long been known, have frequently come up with a kind of morose and mawkish catch-phrase: "I won't see them play in the top-flight division in England in my lifetime." Sadly, it has become true for so many of them. The hope that is supposed to spring eternal has gradually been eroded. The good times have so often been transitory and all too brief: instead there have been times when Hull City have locally been closer to becoming a proverbial music-hall joke.

For all the promise and aspirations they have never been in the top flight – either the old First Division or the newer FA Premiership. But they have been in the old Fourth Division and are in the present Third Division. As the last year of the 20th century dawned, there was a distinct danger that they might even tumble out of the Football League completely – a big-city club in theory only. They have carried on most of their football existence in what were once known as the Second Division, the Third Division and the Third Division North. But in the latter years of the 20th century it has got worse rather than better. No-one seems to have had the perspicacity, intuition or financial clout to deliver the goods to the public on a consistent basis.

One reason for it all might be Hull's geography, but it might also be a ready-made excuse, too. Hull is a big city, but to all intents and purposes it leads nowhere – with the greatest of respect to Spurn Point. It has traditionally been described as being 40 miles down a railway siding. Its isolation has been far from splendid. Lack of self-belief might lie within its introspection in general and Hull City may have merely epitomised it all.

The big-city tag is grossly misleading anyway. What happens in practice is all that really matters. Never mind the possibilities that might have been at City's disposal: the reality is that with monotonous regularity they have been overtaken by clubs with lesser pedigrees and pretensions. Wimbledon, for example, seem to survive comfortably enough in the FA Premiership even though they have so far had only a relatively-brief Football League shelf life. For a few hypnotic days in 1974 that geographical soccer outpost of Carlisle United topped the old First Division, while London clubs such as Leyton Orient and Millwall, neither of whom would have ever been traditionally classified as regular big-time Charlies in footballing parlance with the greatest of respect to them and their achievements, have sampled life in the top flight. Clubs from places such as Watford, Blackburn, Burnley, Bury, Luton, Swindon, Northampton, Preston, Swansea, Oxford and Grimsby, all of whom have a considerably smaller population and hinterland on which to call than Hull, have also done so.

Faced with such statistics, it is little wonder that rather unsavoury arguments, which would seek to deny the adage of "live and let live," continue to prevail that Hull is a rugby-league city and not a soccer one. There are more important things to worry about than something which it is just about impossible to quantify definitively in any case, but the concept belies a moot point.

And not only have Hull City failed to achieve top-flight soccer divisionally: they have also never been to Wembley. For most of the 20th century it was an honour for players to play under the imposing Twin Towers: it was also a comparative rarity. But the changing structure of League soccer has given many more players the chance to fulfil their Wembley dreams than ever before. Once you had to reach an FA Cup Final or play in an international to have your best chance of playing at Wembley. But then there was the Football League Cup, too, and other FA competitions for different divisions and the Finals of the notorious Play-offs. The scope may have been increased and far more players then ever before can nowadays say that they have played at Wembley. Most League clubs have now been to Wembley under one guise or another: Hull City, though, are not surprisingly an exception to the rule.

It is easy to be known as a harbinger of doom and gloom in such circumstances, but it is entirely disappointing and soul-destroying for anyone from Hull with a true passion for soccer. Flattering to deceive has become an art form: it is reality according to the facts and not just a prejudiced opinion.

Yet everything was far more buoyant in the early part of the century when soccer was finally established in the city of Hull in the face of strong competition from rugby league. The Hull City club came into being in their accepted form on June 28, 1904, after two groups had embarked on the venture unknown to each other. They pooled their resources after an application to join the Midland League had not succeeded and the pioneers of the club included chairman William Gilyott, vice-chairman George Lilley, secretary Ben Crompton, John Ramster, Marcus Andrews, Ben Frost, James Barraclough, Arnold Levitt, John Bielby, John Emmerson, Thomas Shaw, William Hay, Richard Hobbs, Ernest Morison, Alfred Spring and Percy Wrightson.

But the company's capital was fixed at only £2,000 in 4,000 ten-shilling shares and there was no rush for them, so some of the directors had to put their hands into their pockets to provide the necessary funds to sustain those early ambitions. It was a taste of things to come at various points in the club's history. City have never continuously been a rich enough club to fulfil their aspirations and their financial standing reached an all-time low when they were forced to go into receivership in February 1982.

But back in 1904-05 City played 44 matches and won 26 of them, failing to score on only three occasions. In fact, they clocked up a total of 115 goals and conceded just 66 in comparison. But they operated from three home bases – the Boulevard, Anlaby Road cricket ground and Dairycoates – and played only 14 away games out of the 44. A total of 28 home games, including the first 20, took place at the Boulevard, the rugby-league home of Hull FC, but the Tigers became decidedly itinerant during March 1905. In a week they beat Scarborough 6-0 at Dairycoates, defeated the Prince of Wales' Hussars 1-0 at the Boulevard and then drew 0-0 with Manchester City at Anlaby Road.

City also had to cede ground advantage to Stockton in their first excursion into the FA Cup because they were only tenants at the Boulevard and "it was a stipulation that fixtures of Hull FC should not be disturbed." During the season they met a number of sides who are scarcely renowned for their soccer prestige nowadays – Denton, Sheffield FC, who are most noted as the oldest club in England, Burton United, Boston Town, Wellingborough, York Garrison, the Prince of Wales' Hussars, the Coldstream Guards, who were hammered 10-3 at the Boulevard, the Army Service Corps, West Hartlepool, Glossop and an East Riding XI. They also played the reserve sides of Manchester City, Gainsborough Trinity and Middlesbrough.

The first game was against Notts County at the Boulevard on September 1, 1904, and it ended in a 2-2 draw with George Rushton scoring City's goals. A week before the game it had been announced that City had decided to play in black-and-amber vertically-striped shirts and two addresses in the city's Washington Street and Brook Street were publicised for any local players who wanted to train with the team. There was naturally great interest as to how the rugby fans would take to the soccer, so the directors thought it might be courteous to help them out and decided "to print off the few important rules and post them prominently on the ground." The crowd came in slowly as the game wore on, but they had swelled to 6,000 by the start of the second half and the gate money amounted to more than £80 with at least £25 being taken in the one-shilling stand. County's team arrived in Hull by train and "were conveyed to the ground by wagonette." The Lord Mayor of Hull was allowed to kick off the game, but it was splendidly reported: "After he had set the leather moving, he seemed inclined to stay in midfield and watch proceedings from there, but a friendly call soon brought him to safety." Presumably, it must go down as the earliest-recorded pitch invasion at a Hull City match!

After that strange opening, the Tigers remained unbeaten for 14 games, mostly at the Boulevard, apart from that first excursion into the FA Cup which ended with an exit against fellow non-League side Stockton. More than anything, it was a season-long prelude to the real thing – League soccer in Hull. That arrived at Anlaby Road cricket ground on September 2, 1905, after the Tigers had been admitted to the Second Division. The visitors were Barnsley and City won 4-1 although it was

Boothferry Park under construction in the summer of 1946.

reported: "It is not their ambition to get near the top in the first season." Unfortunately, a lot of fans have been left waiting for something exceptional to happen ever since...

It did not take City long to make an impact in their first League game because Scottish inside-forward George Spence scored for them after just two minutes. Barnsley were soon level, but City, who had the wind at their backs, were 2-1 ahead by halftime after Davy Gordon had taken David "Soldier" Wilson's pass and carved a way through. The action came thick and fast early in the second half and the crowd were naturally amused by an incident in which a clearance by Gordon struck a police officer in the face and knocked off his helmet. And after Barnsley had hit the woodwork, Wilson made it 3-1 with a shot from a tight angle. Soon afterwards Gordon received an arm injury, but he recovered sufficiently to complete the scoring ten minutes from the end and give City a 4-1 triumph.

City finished fifth in the Second Division in that inaugural season, but they had been forced to play their home games at three different venues – the Boulevard, Anlaby Road cricket ground and eventually Anlaby Road football ground. The three-year tenancy that City's directors had negotiated with Hull FC was terminated before the end of the first season because the Northern Rugby Union's authorities did not allow any club under their jurisdiction from benefiting from such an arrangement. As a result, the Tigers took temporary quarters on Hull Cricket Club's enclosure at Anlaby Road, which was generously placed at their disposal while the

Volunteers from Hull City Supporters' Club help out with work on Boothferry Park just before the ground opened.

ground near the railway was prepared for soccer. And in 1906-07 City played all but two of their home games at Anlaby Road football ground and used the Boulevard only for their clashes with such diverse soccer names as Manchester United and Glossop North End.

The Anlaby Road ground served its purpose until World War Two, withstanding damage from high winds and also a fire during Easter 1914. But the club suffered financial problems leading up to World War Two and then the ground was badly damaged at the height of the Blitz. As a result, the club underwent considerable change and they moved to Boothferry Park, opening it on August 31, 1946, for a goalless draw against Lincoln City. Even then things might have been very different and the Tigers might have ended up playing on the other side of the city.

Local accountant Dick Smith had wanted to reorganise the club and in the end his main support came from builder Harold Needler, who suggested the idea of getting the backing of Kenneth Percival, at that time the Sheriff of Hull, and installing him as the president. Eventually Needler's brothers John and Henry came on board with them.

But Harold Needler's plans had been to create a model garden city in the Sutton area of Hull, including a sports stadium as one of the main amenities within the development. He wanted to form a new soccer club as part of the project, but there was a problem in obtaining League membership. The most viable alternative was to take over the existing Hull City, who lacked a suitable ground, so they made an offer

Hull City fans do a spot of weeding on the Boothferry Park pitch shortly before the opening of the ground.

to buy their assets on the understanding that they would go into voluntary liqui-dation. And after everything had been agreed at an extraordinary general meeting of the old company, a new one came into being with the old name.

Harold Needler's longer-term dream for Boothferry Park initially included an 80,000 capacity with everyone under cover, a possible secondary access to Hessle Road and a railway station to the ground. Not everything worked out quite as intended, but the improvements included four covered sides with the South Stand replacing the popular Bunker's Hill terracing, the promised railway station and six new floodlight pylons with the previous 96-lamp installation being moved up the coast to Scarborough in 1964. A year earlier Needler had also ploughed £200,000 worth of shares into the club to justify his place in the club's history as a genuine benefactor. He was generally popular with the players, who knew him as "Big H," and his death in July 1975 was to prove a watershed in City's fortunes because Don Robinson has been the only subsequent chairman to be as forward-thinking – in his own more flamboyant style – and successful.

And the wheel has rotated full circle in terms of grounds because there has been increasing speculation towards the end of the 20th century that, much to the chagrin of most of the fans, City may end up playing soccer at the Boulevard again. It has been anathema amid mounting speculation about the provision of a super stadium that would house the Tigers and possibly the rugby-league clubs of Hull FC and Hull Kingston Rovers. The public have largely favoured either Boothferry Park or a new super stadium – and nothing else. But the problem has been that

The shell of a stand is in place as Boothferry Park is built in 1946.

Volunteers help to clear the snow from Boothferry Park in February 1947.

Boothferry Park has been allowed to decay in places – almost on a par with the club's fortunes on the field.

The club, therefore, have veered from the sublime to the ridiculous without ever fulfilling their big-city potential. They can bask in the glory of a record 11-1 win over Carlisle United at Anlaby Road on January 14, 1939, or reflect ruefully on a record 8-0 defeat away to Wolverhampton Wanderers on November 4, 1911.

The 11-1 win over Carlisle included six different goalscorers – a hat-trick for Bill Dickinson, two apiece for Arthur Cunliffe, an inspirational left-winger on the day, Dai Davies and Cliff Hubbard and one for both Charlie Robinson and George

Preparations take place for Hull City's biggest-ever crowd of 55,019 for an FA Cup tie against Manchester United in February 1949. A bulldozer works on the extension to Bunker's Hill, while workmen finish the protective fencing near the railway embankment.

Boothferry Park as it looked in the summer of 1952.

Richardson. The Tigers were 4-1 up at halftime and Richardson was making his home debut after a long spell on the injury list – so he presumably thought at the time that every game at Anlaby Road went as smoothly! The thrashing at Wolves involved an amazing irony because Jack Needham and Billy Halligan scored hat-tricks that day – and then joined the Tigers later in their careers. Halligan even scored four goals in a game for City – at home to Wolves in a 7-1 win on December 6, 1913! And to be fair to the Tigers in that 8-0 debacle, they were down to nine fit men after being handicapped by injuries to Joe "Stanley" Smith and William "Tim" Wright, who was apparently kicked on the ankle by the Revd Kenneth Hunt! City presumably knew by then that they just did not have a prayer…

All clubs have, of course, had their loyal servants and Andy Davidson – mainly a wing-half, occasionally even a centre-half or a centre-forward and increasingly a full-back – stands out in Hull City's case. He holds the club record in terms of League appearances – 520 – and his distinguished service also bears testimony to what might have been and what nearly was.

A relative of the famed footballing Shankly family in Scotland, Davidson, also known as either "Drew" or "Jock," was as tough as they come, as anyone ever tackled by him would readily assert. He tells one wonderful story about a bet that he seemingly struck up with his fellow full-back Dennis Butler in one game when they were due to come up against Swindon Town's dangerous wingers Mike Summerbee and Don Rogers. It was a question of who would "subdue" his opposite winger first and any gambler would have placed his money on the more forceful Davidson. But Davidson had to settle for some verbal sparring that apparently led to Rogers playing somewhere behind his own left-back so that he could not get near him. His problem was that in the first attack of the game there was suddenly a commotion on the other side of the field, the outcome of which was that Butler triumphantly claimed his winnings while Summerbee received treatment!

Normally, though, Davidson's rigorous single-mindedness shone through in a different way because he suffered three broken legs of his own early in his career

Re-seeding takes place at Boothferry Park during the early part of the close season in 1956. On the roller are (left to right): Jimmy Lodge, Stan Coombs and Cliff Woodhead.

A tiger goes on parade for Hull City's FA Cup tie against Fulham at Craven Cottage in January 1960.

and it was only his innate resilience that enabled him to battle back from the adversity each time. There was also a serious knee injury before an Achilles tendon problem brought the curtain down on his playing career in 1967. But if he had not had such setbacks, then his appearance record with the Tigers would have been even more exceptional.

In another context, however, there nearly was no record at all. Davidson followed his elder brother, David, to Boothferry Park from their native Lanarkshire in the late 1940s, but he was homesick and it took all of manager Major Frank Buckley's powers of persuasion to make him change his mind about going back to Scotland permanently. He later reflected: "I didn't particularly want to leave home, but big brother said:'Come to England' and in our family what big brother said went. But I could not understand half of what the people in Hull said and I'm sure they didn't know what I was saying. I had no friends of my own age, so back home I went."

But he returned to include a run of 202 consecutive first-team appearances in his loyal service before staying on to help out on the coaching staff when his playing days finally ended. Amid it all, Davidson, always a man with a big heart, is the antithesis of the so-called mean Scot: by nature, he is generous to a fault in all aspects of his life. And he has remained peerless as a thoroughly entertaining raconteur about much of City's postwar soccer. For example, a committee meeting of the

The South Stand begins to replace the popular Bunker's Hill terracing at Boothferry Park during the summer of 1965.

The North Stand at Boothferry Park is knocked down to make way for terracing and a supermarket in January 1982.

Ex-Tigers' Association, who work on behalf of the club's former players, is not complete without a treasured fund of some of Andy's anecdotes. The stories almost seem to get better and sometimes they seem to be even funnier: they are never dull.

But the manner of Davidson's departure from the backroom staff in December 1980 understandably broke his footballing heart. He had a reputation as something of a soccer hard man, but it probably hurt him much more than he would ever publicly confess although he outwardly remained remarkably resilient about the whole messy business. After all, it was an approach that he had had to learn to cultivate towards the setbacks that he had frequently faced during his playing career. And

**The long-serving
Andy Davidson,
pictured in 1957.**

as he tried to come to terms with life without Hull City, he would say almost nonchalantly that he was making the most of the chance to catch up on the two Gs – golfing and gardening. And at one stage he took on a fish round amid the villages to the west of Hull, he was left with a list of potential customers and he found to his disbelief that it was headed by Bob Chapman, the chairman who had sacked him. Davidson was naturally asked about what happened to the Chapman family's fish and no-one was ever too sure as to whether he was serious or jocular when he replied: "I did the only thing I could do with it – I stuck it through the letter-box!"

The cliche of being "Hull City through and through" has been used about too many people who have not remotely deserved it. Andy Davidson undeniably merited it more than most, though, and the way in which the club repaid his loyalty – as the long-serving Billy Bly had also found to his cost – may go some way towards explaining why they have never fulfilled their ambitions.

Chris Chilton, born in the Holderness village of Sproatley, stands as Hull City's

Andy Davidson suffers one of his serious injury setbacks. He is helped along the platform of Hull's Paragon Station by teammates Doug Clarke (left) and Bill Bradbury (right) on their return from a match against Swindon Town in September 1958.

record goalscorer of all time with a tally of 193 in the League between 1960 and 1971 and remains as one of the greatest heroes in the club's history because he was also a successful coach at Boothferry Park in the 1980s. As a player, he had extraordinary heading ability and was one of those big strikers who could seemingly hang in the air as the crosses came over. But just to describe him as a big centre-forward is detrimental to his all-round capabilities. He was strong and powerful, he could lead a line with industry, authority and determination and he was equally adept on the ground.

Chilton's marksmanship twice brought him four goals in a game – against Wrexham in 1963 and Barnsley in 1964 – as well as eight hat-tricks. But he had an almost matter-of-fact modesty towards scoring because he reflected: "People talk about the goals, but I honestly don't think about them. I know there were strikes and there were a lot of headers, but I can hardly remember any of them. There were one or two goals when I did quite well, but there was nothing special. Scoring goals was just part of doing my job."

City were to have some notable double acts in terms of goalscorers. There were, for example, Bill McNaughton and Russell Wainscoat with 62 between them in the 1932-33 season and Bill Bradbury and Colin Smith with 56 between them in the 1958-59 promotion season. But no City twin spearhead can match the longevity of Chris Chilton's partnership with Ken Wagstaff as they terrorised defences together from 1964 to 1971. They scored 52 between them in the 1965-66 season when the other regular members of the forward-line – Ray Henderson, Ken Houghton and Ian Butler – all got into double figures as well and they set a club record of 109 League goals in a season on their way to the Third Division title. But Chilton and Wagstaff had scored 50 League goals between them the previous season – and Wagstaff had not arrived at the club until the November of 1964. And they scored a total of more than 30 goals in every subsequent season together bar one when Chilton missed almost half the campaign because of injury.

Hull City's greatest goalscorer, Chris Chilton.

Chris Chilton scored all four goals for Hull City in their 4-2 home win over Wrexham in October 1963. In this instance he shows his aerial power to score the second of them.

Hull City's lethal striker Ken Wagstaff beats a top-class goalkeeper, former England international Alan Hodgkinson, in a 1-1 draw with Sheffield United at Boothferry Park in October 1970.

The deadly duo were to score 366 League goals between them for the Tigers and Chilton wryly remarked that the tally might have been much higher: "I'm always surprised nowadays about what seem to me to be own goals, which strikers claim for themselves. If we'd been given them when we played, I reckon that Ken Wagstaff and I would have had about a thousand between us! There must have been lots more of mine which were own goals then, but would be accredited to me now. It doesn't niggle me, but it's the one thing I can't comprehend in football now."

Neither should Chilton ever being underestimated in terms of his leadership qualities because he was to captain Hull City towards the end of his career at Boothferry Park. And those people who might claim that a centre-forward should not captain a side because of positional or tactical reasons had never seen Chilton lead from the front by example.

His qualities were epitomised by successive home games a little more than halfway through the 1970-71 season. On Boxing Day, 1970, a crowd of 24,399

Two of Hull City's all-time greats, Raich Carter (left) with his protege Ken Wagstaff.

started to watch the Tigers play Sheffield Wednesday, but soon drifted away in their hordes. As one of the City players, Malcolm Lord, recalled: "Wednesday had three shots at goal and a penalty and found themselves 4-1 up, but then we scored three goals in seven minutes near the end. The pity was that most of our fans had gone home by then." But the fightback, arguably one of the most memorable in City's history, was inspired by Chilton's never-say-die attitude. He scored twice, Ken Wagstaff grabbed another and City had claimed an unlikely 4-4 draw. The Tigers' next League game was against Sunderland and Chilton scored one of his hat-tricks with another inspired and inspiring performance in a 4-0 victory. His second goal was a glancing header from a cross by Ian Butler and even Chilton remembers it well: "I had to arch backwards to flick it and when it went in at the far post, it was just right." His all-round public esteem as one of the club's all-time heroes was probably never higher even though he will be always closely associated with the goals that flowed during the 1965-66 promotion season.

It is a fitting tribute to the partnership between Chris Chilton and Ken Wagstaff that they are comfortably the Tigers' top goalscorers of all time. Wagstaff, after all, is comfortably second in the record scoring stakes behind Chilton with 173 League goals for City to his credit. A lethal goal-poacher, he was never flustered when a chance fell to him and Andy Davidson, his captain during the 1965-66 promotion season, always stressed that most strikers tended to panic in front of goal, but Wagstaff was the opposite because he remained cool, calm and collected and almost put the pressure back on to the defenders to stop him.

Wagstaff himself pays tribute to Raich Carter, another of City's all-time greats who was his manager during his formative years with Mansfield Town, and Cliff Britton, who was in charge at Boothferry Park during the glory years of the 1960s, for their ability to develop his positional sense. But he otherwise insists that goalscorers are born and not made: "I don't think that goalscoring can be taught because it's an instinct. It is a gift. When you're in the penalty area, you mustn't panic, but you should take your time. You must be good positionally and you don't need to belt the ball into the net when you can side-foot it. I never feared any goalkeeper and you can't afford to. I enjoyed scoring against top-drawer international goalkeepers such as Peter Bonetti at Chelsea, Gordon Banks against Stoke City and

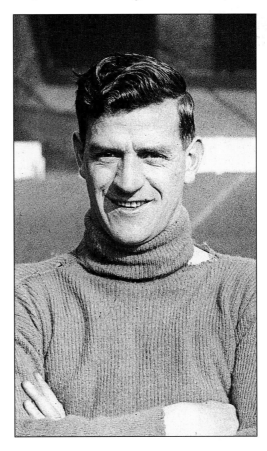

Peter Shilton against Leicester City. You miss some chances, but if you keep trying to take them, then you'll always score your fair share. And that's why you must keep going when things aren't going well because if you do, it all comes back in the end and you start scoring again."

Hull City have also had a reputation for producing outstanding goalkeepers of their own and none can match the longevity of Billy Bly, who served the club from 1937 to 1960. Bly, who was from the Walker area of Newcastle, made 403 League appearances for City, but for two reasons there has always been speculation as to what might have been. His tally of appearances would have been far higher if it had not been for the interruption caused by World War Two

Hull City's stalwart goalkeeper George "Geordie" Maddison.

and the number of serious injuries that he incurred. Bly, who died in March 1982, was not big for a goalkeeper, but he was spectacularly brave at times and it was estimated that he suffered 14 fractures during his career. He was carried off after a collision in the first game at Boothferry Park against Lincoln City in 1946 and even when he earned an England B international call-up, he broke his arm and had to forfeit his big chance. But it is a testimony to Bly's ability and subsequent popularity with the public that he played in two promotion seasons for the Tigers ten years apart – in 1948-49 and 1958-59 – and Denis Durham was the only other player to achieve that notable feat alongside him.

For a while Bly ran a highly-successful confectionery shop close to Boothferry Park after his retirement and it always seemed to do a roaring trade on match days. It was once said that he was the third most popular man in Hull after the Lord Mayor and Raich Carter. The legendary Carter, also a shopkeeper a bit further from the ground on the city's Anlaby Road at one stage, said of Bly: "I don't think City will have ever had a finer goalkeeper. He was consistent and never let us down. More than that, he was a very good chap off the field. He was amiable, good company and a joy to be with."

Bly remains the longest-serving player in the club's history and was a natural successor in some ways to George "Geordie" Maddison, another goalkeeper and another loyal servant. Their paths at the club briefly crossed and Maddison is second behind Andy Davidson in the number of League games that he started for the club – 430. It has to be said, though, that Garreth Roberts, a pocket battleship of a midfield dynamo who led the Tigers to two promotions in the 1980s, played in 461 League games. But these include 414 starts and 47 appearances as a substitute, so the statisticians of the modern era will probably put Roberts second behind Davidson and Maddison in third place, just ahead of Bly, in the all-time lists.

Maddison had a lot in common with Bly. He, too, was from the North-East, as his nickname would indicate. He came from Birtley in County Durham and had an

Hull City's record-breaking Welsh international goalkeeper Tony Norman.

Hull City's loyal servant Billy Bly beats Plymouth Argyle's inside-forward Wilf Carter to a cross in a 3-1 win at Boothferry Park in August 1959. Bly's teammates Brian Garvey (left) and Paul Feasey (right) provide extra cover.

extravagant style at times – he would commentate on the proceedings to fans who congregated behind his goal and he was known to venture well outside his penalty area when he thought that circumstances dictated it. He would throw sweets to youngsters behind his goal and on one bitterly cold day a group of supporters provided him with a brazier to keep him warm! Like Bly, he also had plenty of injury setbacks during his career and one too many finished him in 1938. Signed from Tottenham Hotspur in the summer of 1924, Maddison was an ever-present in City's goal between February 14, 1925, and November 16, 1927: neither did he miss a League game during the 1933-34 and 1936-37 seasons. He was also a good singer and died in Hull Royal Infirmary in May 1959 after collapsing on stage at the city's Manor Club. Bly fittingly reflected: "He passed on plenty of tips to me, especially with regard to angles. We did all our training together. He was a grand chap."

But no-one can match the feat of another City goalkeeper, Tony Norman, who holds the club record of 226 League appearances. The sequence began on August 27, 1983, in a home game against Burnley, whose side included Lee Dixon, later to become one of Arsenal's famed back-four. More ironic was the fact that Norman's run was just starting and left-back Kim Wassell played in the same game, but he never started another League game for the Tigers even though they won 4-1 that day, so he must surely count as one of the club's most successful players of all time! Norman's run ended, meanwhile, when he had a neck injury and Gavin Kelly replaced him in a 2-2 draw at Oldham Athletic on September 24, 1988.

Norman, a Welsh international who became a police officer when his playing days were over, still marvels as to how he managed to set the record because he recalled: "I think it was all a bit daft on occasions because John Davies, our other goalkeeper, damaged his cruciate knee ligaments in a reserve game and was out for a long time. We didn't have another experienced 'keeper at the time, so it became a case of just having to get on with it even when I picked up a few niggles. I think it happened a couple of times, but they would just bandage you up and out you'd go again. On one occasion I hurt my back in training and if there'd been another ready-made 'keeper available, I'd have dropped out, but I didn't. Yet I couldn't even bend down to tie up my boots – someone else had to do it for me! It was just a question of getting through the game and just hoping that everything didn't suddenly go pear-shaped, but it was absolutely crackers really. At the same time we were doing well and had gone up from the old Fourth Division and the Third Division and then finished sixth in our first season in the Second Division. The spirit was so good then, we'd had a bit of success and I think my situation became part of our desire to keep things going."

There have, therefore, been some good, old days in City's history, but there have been some bad times, too. In the League they have been promoted six times and relegated on eight occasions. But in cup ties they have been giantkillers much more often than they have been giantkilled. And although there may not really have been the good, the bad and the ugly, there has certainly been the bizarre to add to the moments of success and failure.

Chapter Two

Stranger than Fiction

HULL City's hopes of fulfilling their potential and joining soccer's elite have usually foundered on the rocks of despair, but along the way they have been involved a number of notable moments. As with most clubs, they have been confronted with all kinds of quirks of fate – some good, some bad – that have contrived to defy the odds. Some have gone into the history-books and some have been heavily dosed in pathos. The common denominator is that they have been outwardly unbelievable or incomprehensible, especially when they have happened to a club whose ultimate objectives have never been reached. In other words, they have been stranger than any football fiction.

City supporters, for example, go into every match in every season defiantly believing against all odds that they their team are the greatest. The fact they have never quite lived up to that billing in reality is not their fault: the blame should be laid at the door of the others who have got in their way and provided insurmountable barriers. But there was a time when the Tigers might arguably have claimed to be greatest in terms of club football. And they did not have to be champions of any division or land any trophy to prove it.

It happened on the spring evening of April 11, 1972, when City played a friendly in front of a crowd of 11,848 at Boothferry Park against a touring team called Nacional from Montevideo. Nacional were undefeated on tour, but that was hardly surprising because they were acknowledged as the world club champions, they had been Uruguayan champions four years in succession and their side included a host of internationals who had played in World Cup tournaments for Brazil, Uruguay and Argentina.

But the Tigers went into a 2-0 lead in the first half when Stuart Pearson stabbed the ball home after a 23rd-minute build-up involving Paul O'Riley, Ian Butler, Ken Houghton, Ken Knighton and Jimmy McGill and then John Kaye cracked a 25-yard

The Hull City party at London's Heathrow Airport as they prepare to fly out to Israel for their end-of-season tour in 1950.

drive into the top corner of the net after 33 minutes. Morales, who had helped Uruguay to the semi-finals of the 1970 World Cup, struck twice early in the second half to make it 2-2, but Houghton then took control. He took O'Riley's pass to put City back in front in the 74th minute, hit the woodwork and then supplied the defensive-splitting ball that enabled Roy Greenwood to score his first senior goal after 84 minutes.

It finished 4-2 and technically City fans could be excused for insisting that their team really were the greatest in view of the status of the opposition. It was some years later, of course, that Don Robinson, by then the club chairman, memorably said that he wanted the Tigers to be the first team to play on the moon. On that night in 1972 City supporters doubtless believed that that was all that was left for them to conquer.

The triumph over Naçional has to be seen in its context, of course, but it was hardly a one-off affair in the Tigers' history. They have done well against some notable foreign sides in their time: normally the games were friendlies, but they have beaten Italian giants Lazio, one of Paul Gascoigne's old clubs, in a competitive match, for example. It happened in the Anglo-Italian Cup in front of a 7,325 crowd at Boothferry Park on February 21, 1973, when City won 2-1 after Ken Knighton and Roy Greenwood had put them in the driving seat with two goals in the opening 23 minutes.

At that time Lazio were emerging from the shadows of local rivals Roma and were top of the league in Italy for the first time for 35 years. Their skipper was the quaintly-named Guiseppe Wilson, who had been born in Darlington of an English father and an Italian mother before his family emigrated while he was still a youngster. But that cup tie was to be remembered for all the wrong reasons and Wilson was involved in one of the biggest skirmishes of all when he was booked for laying out City's burly striker Phil Holme with what was described as "a wrestler's throw." And while Holme was prone, there was a punch-up around him that led to City's assistant manager Wilf Dixon and substitute Ian McKechnie going on to the pitch. In another clash City's striker Stuart Pearson was booked by Italian referee Cesare Gussoni after an incident 70 yards away from the ball, while a policeman had to intervene when one of the Boothferry Park stewards was doused with a sponge from the Lazio dug-out. City's manager Terry Neill tried to put everything into its rightful context afterwards when he maintained: "This was quite mild compared with what it can be like against Italians." He had, after all, just left Highbury to join City as their player-manager in 1970 when Arsenal were involved in a street brawl with Lazio after an Inter-Cities' Fairs Cup tie…

The Tigers can also reflect on some impressive friendly results against other crack European sides. At various times they have beaten Sparta Rotterdam, Galatasaray, Vasas, IFK Stockholm, Banik Ostrava and European Cup Finalists Bruges and SV Werder Bremen as well as drawing with Malmo FF and Kaiserslautern. And even though they have lost to big clubs such as Slovan Bratislava, Athletic Bilbao, Atletico Madrid, Partizan Belgrade, Fiorentina and Dinamo Kiev on other occasions on which they have pitted their wits against lead-

Hull City striker Paul O'Riley scores in a 1-1 draw with German side FC Kaiserlautern at Boothferry Park in August 1972.

The popular Stan Mortensen.

ing European opposition in friendlies, they have also in their time beaten so-called international XIs from countries such as Belgium, French Guiana, Guyana, Trinidad and Tobago, Japan and Israel and drawn with Bermuda.

And for all their ultimate lack of achievement, City can also claim to have some of the greatest players in world football in their ranks at some time. That is because they have frequently signed former internationals in the twilight of their careers and the list is impressive in any football quarters. It includes Jack Hill, Neil Franklin, Stan Mortensen, Willie Buchan, Jackie Sewell, Wilf Mannion, Peter Barnes, Billy Bremner, Emlyn Hughes and George Cummins.

Some of them such as Jackie Sewell still talk fondly of their time at Boothferry Park and ask about the whereabouts of some of their former teammates and George Cummins has travelled across the country to attend old players' reunions in Hull, while Stan Mortensen was a particularly popular figure in the City dressing-room. A wonderful character, he would almost poignantly proclaim without a tinge of malice towards Stan Matthews: "I'm the only player to score a hat-trick in an FA Cup Final and have the game named after someone else!" He once had a job as a hosiery salesman and told me proudly: "I travel in ladies' underwear, you know!" Bob Dennison recalls how "Morty" checked as to which of his City teammates had children and would then turn up with sticks of rock for them from his base in Blackpool. And Brian Bulless remembers how he would not arrive in the dressing-room until about 20 minutes before kick-off time at Boothferry Park, the door would then suddenly burst open and a voice would boom: "Never fear, Morty's here!"

Conversely, others such as long-throw expert Sam Weaver, England manager Don Revie, Sheffield Wednesday's FA Cup winning captain Ronnie Starling, Stuart Pearson, Douglas "Dally" Duncan and Brian Marwood played for the club in the formative part of their careers before becoming full internationals. It may never have brought Hull City the lasting achievements that they have long desired, but it does pose intriguing thoughts about the make-up of the club's greatest-ever team. It is always a matter of opinion and something that cannot easily be quantified. But is it based on the players who have contributed most to their side's well-being at the height of their powers or is it based on the players who have represented the club even if they have found greater fame and esteem elsewhere?

It also brings up the topic of the ones who got away. Most clubs lose players from their own environs for various reasons at various times – it is an infuriating fact of soccer life – but occasionally outsiders are involved at a club for

a time and then somehow slip the net. As with most clubs, it has happened to the Tigers.

One of the first instances in City's history concerned a full-back called Doug Gray, who played in one trial match as a 19-year-old against Corinthians at Anlaby Road on December 19, 1924. Corinthians were leading 4-1 when the game was abandoned after 85 minutes after their centre-forward E. R. M. Hilleary had broken his leg in a collision with City goalkeeper Harry Dyke. Gray, who had previously been with Aberdeen Mugiemoss, never reappeared in the Tigers' colours, but he did well for himself because six months later he joined Glasgow Rangers, whom he helped to ten Scottish titles and six Scottish FA Cup triumphs, and played for them

Hull City duo Brian Garvey (left) and Brian Bulless test out a frozen Boothferry Park during the big freeze of 1963.

until October 1945. Gray, who later had a coaching stint with Clyde, also went on to win ten caps as a Scottish international.

Goalkeeper Ted Sagar earned a place for himself in soccer's record-books for spending the longest time – 24 years – as a player with one professional club, Everton. He won two League titles and was an FA Cup winner as well being capped by England four times. Sagar retired in 1953, having joined the Toffeemen in March 1929. Yet four months earlier he had been an 18-year-old trialist with the Tigers while he was with his local club, Thorne Colliery. City's only compensation was that a few years later they began to be well-served by another legendary goalkeeper, Billy Bly, who was with the club for 22 years.

Then there was Kevin Hector, who won First Division titles with Derby County and made two brief England appearances. He had a trial with the Tigers when Bob Brocklebank was their manager and was highly recommended after it, but the club were unable to take on any more professionals at the time and he was allowed to drift away. Hector later recalled: "I was 16 at the time and played on either the left-wing or the right-wing, but obviously Hull City could-n't have thought much about me. I then had trials with Bradford and they signed me. Apart from Bradford, Hull City were the only other club with whom I had trials." The curious postscript is that when Brocklebank later became manager of Bradford City, he tried to sign Hector from Bradford Park Avenue, who were then, of course, still a League club.

More recently young defender Michael Clegg was on schoolboy forms with the Tigers, but was allowed to leave. He is originally from Ashton-under-Lyne and has since broken through into League soccer on several occasions just a few miles down down the road – in Manchester United's first team.

But probably the classic example concerns Stuart Pearce, who did wear the amber and black of Hull City as a teenager before going on to an illustrious career with England, Coventry City, Nottingham Forest, Newcastle United and West Ham United. Mike Smith was the Tigers' manager at the time and he brought in two trial-ists from non-League Wealdstone, Pearce and England non-League international John Watson. Pearce played for City's reserves in a 1-1 draw against their Grimsby Town counterparts at Blundell Park on October 6, 1980. Andy Flounders put the Tigers ahead, Dean Crombie equalised for the Mariners and the game was played in torrential rain at times. It is not known whether a wet night in Grimsby put Pearce off in any way, but he is, of course, renowned as a man of strong will and character, so it is probably true that he had a good job outside soccer and did not want to commit himself to the game as a professional at that time.

But, for a club who have never been among soccer's elite, Hull City have had their moments when they can stake some claims to have been part of the game's history.

One such incident occurred on the night of August 5, 1970, when the Tigers entertained Manchester United in front of 34,007 fans at Boothferry Park. The two sides were meeting in the Watney Cup, basically a pre-season tournament of the day for the highest goalscorers who had not earned honours in the four divisions during the previous campaign.

That season City won 4-0 at Peterborough United with two goals apiece by

Hull City goalkeeper Ian McKechnie beats Manchester United's Brian Kidd to a cross in the Watney Cup tie at Boothferry Park in August 1970.

Chris Chilton and Ken Wagstaff in their first match in the competition. Four days later they faced the Reds at the semi-final stage and drew 1-1 with them. Chris Chilton put City ahead after 11 minutes, but Denis Law equalised for United in the 78th minute. Extra time brought no more goals, so the game had to be decided on penalties – the first domestic competitive game in England to go to a shoot-out because it had been in only the close season that FIFA had decided to outlaw the practice of tossing a coin to determine the outcome of drawn cup ties.

Such was the nature of the sides that two England internationals, City's Stuart Pearson and United's Nobby Stiles, were on the substitutes' bench that night and the list of penalty-takers included some of the most famous names in the respective clubs' history. The penalty shoot-out began with George Best, Brian Kidd and Bobby Charlton scoring for United and Terry Neill, Ian Butler and Ken Houghton replying for the Tigers. It was then that fate dictated that City goalkeeper Ian McKechnie should forever be associated with that first penalty shoot-out.

McKechnie became the first goalkeeper to save a penalty in a shoot-out when he denied Law, but Wagstaff shot wide and the chance to seize the initiative had gone. Willie Morgan put the Reds 4-3 ahead and then McKechnie also became the first player to lose a penalty shoot-out for his side – an ironic outcome because people normally think that goalkeepers can only be heroes in such situations. McKechnie, once a left-winger in his early days with Arsenal, rattled the bar with his penalty and the Tigers were out.

What made it such a difficult pill for City to swallow was the notion that they should have been awarded a penalty in the 88th minute of the game itself when Wagstaff went down heavily following a challenge by United's goalkeeper Alex Stepney. Wagstaff was in no doubt about the decision that should have ensued because he said:"Apparently the referee thought I would not have got to the ball, but I could hardly get to it because I was lying on the ground."

McKechnie, meanwhile, paid the price for showing a willingness to accept the responsibility of taking a penalty in a shoot-out. And he recalled: "I knew Alex Stepney from when he was at Millwall and I was with Arsenal and Southend United and there was some talk about goalkeepers always being the heroes and never the villains in such circumstances. But I never quite figured out why I took the vital penalty. For the previous two weeks we'd practised taking penalties in every training session, but I wasn't supposed to take one. The trouble was that once there was a match situation, everyone else bottled it. I told John McSeveney, who was then the coach, and he said:'Don't be so stupid.' But when it came to it, no-one else would take it. Alex asked: 'What are you doing?' when I started walking back with him towards the goal where the penalties were being taken. I said I was taking one against him and he said:'You're joking!' It might have worked or I might have hit the corner flag – as it was, I hit the bar. And none of the City players talked to me afterwards because I'd lost them their win bonus. They blamed me even though I was the only one who'd take it. And the daft thing was that we'd had a blatant penalty turned down in the first 90 minutes."

McKechnie was one of City's larger-than-life characters in true goalkeeping tradition – he used to collect oranges thrown to him by fans and once entranced a group of mature ladies in Torquay with some flamboyant high kicking as he fooled them into thinking that he was Frankie Vaughan – and he did score twice for the club. On both occasions – in Chris Chilton's testimonial match against Leeds United in 1971 and against a Berbice FA XI in 1973 – he had been used as a substitute and gone on as an outfield player.

And in one of the first friendlies in City's history, they won 4-1 at Sparta Rotterdam on a two-match Dutch tour in May 1910. Joe "Stanley" Smith scored twice for City, Anthony "Andy" Browell was also on the mark and goalkeeper Teddy Roughley also got in on the act. When the Tigers were awarded a penalty, he raced downfield to take it and scored as what he saw as some strange ritual of revenge! Conversely, the Tigers' George Maddison saved a penalty taken by his opposite number Charles Dennington in a 5-2 win in a benefit match at Norwich on April 19, 1926. It was a strange occasion anyway because the game was to raise funds on behalf of Norwich City captain George Martin – and the Tigers' line-up included a different George Martin...

And another long-serving City goalkeeper Tony Norman can boast a goalscoring feat when he played in an end-of season, fund-raising friendly against Kilham at Rudston in May 1988. But he actually started

Hull City's innovative goalkeeper Tony Norman.

the game as a goalkeeper and then decided to have a stint as an outfield player as it wore on, promptly scoring in a 10-0 victory.

But neither McKechnie, who had also scored for Arsenal's third team with one of his famed long kicks down the middle, Roughley nor Norman could match the exploits of the Tigers' Northern Ireland international goalkeeper Alan Fettis. Steve Wilson was in City's goal for their League game at home to Oxford United on December 17, 1994, and Fettis was on the substitutes' bench. But ten minutes from the end Fettis was brought on in place of Linton Brown as an outfield player and in the 88th minute he responded by scoring the final goal in a 3-1 victory from Craig Lawford's cross. He reflected: "After a couple of minutes I'd done a few flicks, made a couple of runs and thought: 'This isn't as easy as it looks.' I was shattered, but then when the ball came across, all I wanted to do was to keep it low and get it on target. Then it hit my heel and bounced into the top corner." Fettis then produced an action replay with another late goal in a 2-1 win at Blackpool on May 6, 1995, but this time he had actually started the game as a striker. In addition, the Seasiders also used two goalkeepers because they had Lee Martin sent off and he was replaced by Mel Capleton…

Another City goalkeeper Jeff Wealands, meanwhile, experienced a different kind of notoriety on September 18, 1973. The Tigers lost 3-1 to Bristol City on a wet and windy night at Ashton Gate and the game was delicately poised at 1-1 until the 55th minute. At that point Bristol's goalkeeper Ray Cashley sent a huge clearance downfield and scored from about 100 yards' range after Wealands had allowed the ball to bounce over his head. Cashley was immediately swamped by his laughing teammates: the embarrassed Wealands was left to beat the ground with his fists in anguish.

Life, therefore, has had some uncanny twists and turns for the Tigers' goalkeepers and after Ian McKechnie's personal drama in 1970, Manchester United went on to lose 4-1 to Derby County in that Watney Cup Final. But the following year City again qualified for the competition and this time they went a stage further. They won 3-0 at Mansfield Town with goals by Chris Galvin, Jimmy McGill and Roy Greenwood and then beat Bristol Rovers at Eastville when Malcolm Lord scored the only goal of the match. That gave City a place in their first domestic Final of any note and nowadays there would be every chance of the game taking place at Wembley. Typical of the Tigers' luck, they merely went to the old Victoria Ground, where they lost 2-0 to Stoke City in the Final on August 18, 1973.

The same kind of situation gave Hull City a piece of unwanted soccer history on May 24, 1984, in what was then known as the Associate Members' Cup and has since reappeared in several different sponsorship-orientated guises. The competition, which developed from the Football League Group Cup and the Football League Trophy, is for clubs in the League's bottom two divisions – or, as someone once asked with a touching mixture of cynicism and accuracy: "How bad do clubs have to be to qualify for it?" Nevertheless, it does give two of them a chance to play at Wembley that they would not normally have. Every Final bar one has taken place at Wembley, but the two Finalists tossed for the choice of home ground for the first one. It involved the Tigers and they ended up playing at Boothferry Park instead of in the shadow of the famous Twin Towers!

City had to play five games to reach that Final – winning 2-1 at York City with goals by Steve McClaren and Alan Taylor, 1-0 at home to Bury with a goal by Stan McEwan, 3-0 at home to Preston North End with two goals by Garreth Roberts and one by Taylor, 1-0 at home to Sheffield United with a goal by Paul Olsson, who never played a League game for the club, and 4-1 at home to Tranmere Rovers with two goals apiece by Taylor and Garreth Roberts. That left them to face AFC Bournemouth, the southern-area winners after beating Millwall 2-1. The Tigers had beaten Bournemouth twice in the League that season and they won the toss of a coin at Football League headquarters to earn the right to have home advantage in the Final.

The Tigers' luck was well and truly out by then, though, because they lost 2-1. Bobby McNeil put City ahead after 21 minutes, but 15 minutes later the Cherries equalised thanks to Milton Graham and in the 73rd minute Paul Morrell grabbed their winner. It was a sad end to the season for the Tigers because they had missed promotion from the old Third Division by a point or a goal and manager Colin Appleton had resigned to join Swansea City, leaving Chris Chilton in charge for the Final. And not surprisingly, the attendance for the clash with Bournemouth was just 6,197 and it remains comfortably the lowest-ever for a Final in the competition because fans do have a habit of emerging from the proverbial woodwork when there is the mouth-watering prospect of a trip to watch their favourites at Wembley instead of Boothferry Park!

That 1983-84 season had also featured another strange incident in City's history because they got themselves into trouble with the soccer powers-that-be for failing to arrive at one of their League games. It happened on January 14, 1984, when the Tigers were scheduled to visit Burnley at Turf Moor. The weather was a mixture of snow, wind and frost as the City party left Boothferry Park on a coach that was barely half-full and its lack of weight meant that it swayed disconcertingly from side to side on the hillier parts of the M62. The blizzard-ridden journey became increasingly tortuous and I can recall skipper Garreth Roberts commenting ominously to me on the fact that Steve McClaren had dropped out of the squad on the morning of the match: "You hear about these disasters when someone escapes because of a twist of fate. The way we're going on, Steve McClaren might be the only one left by Monday, so he may have to take over as manager…"

As it was, manager Colin Appleton exchanged some hectic telephone calls with his Burnley counterpart John Bond from Hartshead Moor services on the M62. And although the Turf Moor pitch was playable, it was decided that it was too dangerous for the City party to carry on with their journey to get there, so they turned round and returned to Hull. As a result, the Football League held an inquiry into the situation and the Tigers were relieved to be fined instead of having any points, which were so vital to their promotion push, deducted. The game was rearranged at the end of the season and City won 2-0, but one more goal would have given them promotion and they missed out. And just for the record, Steve McClaren has survived, or course, to become Manchester United's assistant manager during their momentous treble season of 1998-99. Furthermore, he still benevolently refers to Colin Appleton as Tractor Man from their time together with the Tigers when the manager was involved in another travelling mishap…

If that were an occasion on which City did not play a game in unusual circumstances, then there was, however, an occasion on which they played two on the same day. Many of today's managers and players seem to complain about fixture congestion at the first opportunity, but such matters were organised very differently in the early part of the 20th century. And the Tigers found themselves in something of a dilemma in their first season in the Football League when they were refused permission to alter a double booking. As a result, they were ordered to play a Second Division game and an FA Cup tie on the same stipulated date – October 28, 1905.

It was only City's second season in the FA Cup and they found themselves drawn away to non-League Denaby United in the second qualifying round after having beaten Grimethorpe United 8-1, which is still their biggest win in the competition, at home. The trouble was that City also had the little matter of a League clash against Manchester United at the Boulevard to contemplate. It was not surprisingly agreed that the first team would meet United and that the Cubs – as the Tigers' reserves were then called – would go to Denaby.

City lost 1-0 to Manchester United amid bizarre circumstances in front of their best home crowd of the season – 12,000 – because Henry Simmon had a possible equaliser controversially disallowed. One of the linesmen ruled that the ball had crossed the line, but he was a City director and stand-in referee Smith overruled him! And the change to the match officials had occurred because referee Strawson had missed his train from Lincoln and did not appear until well into the second half.

But it turned out to be a more satisfactory day for the reserves at Midland League Denaby, whose side were described as "a heavyish lot who gave the Cubs a stone-and-a-half per man." In addition, the fixture pile-up meant that City's Patrick Lavery, who was to be killed in action in World War One, lined up against his cousin. City travelled by train to Conisbrough for the game, stopping off for dinner at Doncaster's Glyn Hotel: Denaby's preparations, though, were less conventional because they had enjoyed a club dinner the night before the match. They ended up being reduced to ten men and the Cubs duly won 2-0 with goals by Jackie Smith in front of a 3,000 crowd to earn themselves a third qualifying round tie at home to the side then known as Leeds City.

The whole situation, though, must have been a trifle annoying for two of City senior players, goalkeeper Martin Spendiff and left-winger Andrew Raisbeck. The double date ultimately meant that they forfeited their chances to be the only ever-presents in the club's 44 League and Cup games. Both played against Manchester United that day and were the only two players to appear in the remaining 43 games in the Tigers' first season as a League club.

In contrast, there was also an occasion on which the Tigers fulfilled a fixture that became known as the game that never was. It did actually take place on the evening of September 2, 1931, but it was later expunged from the records. City began the 1931-32 season in the Third Division North with a 1-0 home win over Halifax Town and then travelled to Wigan Borough for their second game of the campaign. They lost 3-1, but on October 26, 1931, Wigan resigned from the League and the game was declared null and void. The return meeting had not taken place, so City played 41 League games that season, but only 40 of them officially counted. For the record, Wigan went 2-0 ahead in the opening 13 minutes and scored a third late on, while

Simon Raleigh, who had scored the winner against Halifax, was on the mark for the Tigers with an opportunist goal in the first half. It was even more disappointing for City centre-half Charles Wrack because he made only three other League appearances for the club.

It all brings to light an anomaly in soccer that Keith Edwards, a regular marksman for the Tigers in two spells with the club, once brought to the fore in a goalscoring context. While reviewing his goalscoring record, he once expressed his annoyance that goals scored in end-of-season Play-offs did not count to his tally. The same, of course, applies to abandoned games – as Denis Law memorably found to his cost in 1961 after scoring six times for Manchester City against Luton Town in an FA Cup tie that lasted only 69 minutes before rain intervened – but, perversely, bookings and sendings-off do count in such instances.

Centre-forward Simon Raleigh, however, was a tragic figure because he died at the age of 24 after playing for Gillingham in their home game against Brighton and Hove Albion on December 1,

Hull City's five-goal hero Simon Raleigh, who died tragically.

1934. Three players died nationally as a result of playing soccer that day and Raleigh initially seemed to have recovered from a collision early in the game. He appeared to be dazed for a while, but said that he was all right at halftime and carried on. But in the second half he collapsed and was rushed to hospital, where he died from a brain haemorrhage without regaining consciousness. The prolific Raleigh had scored 61 goals in a season as an amateur for Silverwood Colliery, later Ken Houghton's first club, and was on the mark 21 times in 31 League appearances for City. He scored five goals in the Tigers' 10-0 victory – still a joint record winning margin for the club in League soccer – over Halifax Town on Boxing Day, 1930. And Ken McDonald is the only City player to perform that feat in a League game because he was on the mark five times in a 5-1 home win over Bristol City on November 17, 1928.

Another ex-Tiger had previously died during a League game, though. It happened on October 27, 1906, when inside-forward David Wilson, who had been nicknamed "Soldier" by City supporters, was playing for the old Leeds City club against Burnley at Elland Road. He is said to have died "from the effects of a charge during the progress of the game." Yet it was called "heart failure from over-exhaustion" at the inquest three days later when, tragically, it was also indicated that if

Wilson had not returned to the field a second time, he would probably have recovered.

Although the circumstances were rather less mawkish, City midfield player George Lyall had an astonishing end to his playing career. He had joined the club from Nottingham Forest for £18,000 in December 1975 after previously playing for

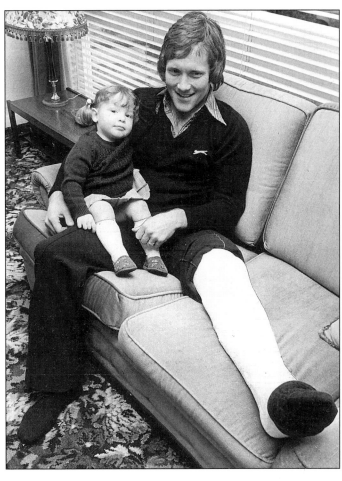

Raith Rovers and Preston North End, but he broke his left leg in a Second Division game against Bolton Wanderers at Boothferry Park on February 19, 1977, and never played again. Lyall was accidentally injured in a challenge involving Bolton's defender Sam Allardyce and it happened just as he was on the mark for City in a 2-2 draw, so he had the rare distinction of being able to say that he scored with his last kick in League soccer. And he admitted: "I knew straightaway that my leg was broken, but I didn't find out that I'd scored as well until I got into the dressing-room. But I suppose that if you leave the game through injury, then the best time to do it is when you've scored."

Les Thompson, a left-sided utility player, left the Tigers in similarly ironic and rare circumstances. After all, he had a record of scoring in his first League game for City and his last. Thompson grabbed the winner with the only goal of the game at home to Ipswich Town on October 10, 1987, and was also on the mark in a 2-1 victory at Newcastle United on May 11, 1991. But the goal at St. James' Park hardly did his career much good – he was given a free transfer at the end of the season!

On a general basis all kinds of significance can be placed on goals scored and conceded by the Tigers during their history. They have come in all shapes and sizes for a start. Take City's

Hull City midfield man George Lyall is pictured with his daughter Louise after breaking his leg while scoring in the 2-2 draw against Bolton Wanderers at Boothferry Park in February 1977.

Hull City's unlucky goalscorer Les Thompson.

Referee Jones receives attention after being knocked out in the build-up to Hull City's goal in a 1-1 draw against Watford at Boothferry Park in December 1964.

28th-minute equaliser in a 1-1 draw against Watford at Boothferry Park on December 12, 1964, for instance. The Hornets' defender Bryn Jones, who had incidentally put them ahead 17 minutes earlier, tried to hack the ball clear when he found himself under pressure in his own penalty area, but it struck the referee, also called Jones, on the back of his head at relatively close quarters and knocked him unconscious. At this point Chris Chilton carried on playing and promptly set up the chance for Ken Wagstaff to score. There was then a dramatic hold-up while the referee received attention and the 6,165 crowd wondered what would happen next. After he had been revived, Mr Jones consulted a linesman and then pointed to the centre-spot to award a goal that he had not seen!

There were also the goals that never were. Controversial moments have played their part at vital stages of City's history and there were three highly-debatable goals – one that suddenly appeared from nowhere in the record-books and two in the 1960s – that annoyed the fans because they believed that they were not actually scored.

The mystery goal concerns City's final match of the 1912-13 season at home to Leicester Fosse on April 26, 1913. It had been preceded by a presentation evening at Hull's Imperial Hotel to manager Ambrose Langley and left-winger Gordon Wright, who were both leaving the club after the clash with Leicester. Langley, who was to take charge of Sheffield Wednesday, was given a smoker's cabinet, while Wright, an amateur who was taking up a post as a mining engineer in South Africa, was presented with a diamond scarf pin and gold cuff links. And after their final game with the club the following day it was reported: "The Tigers wound up their season with a two-goal victory over Leicester." Both goals were scored by Alf Fenwick, it was to all intents and purposes a 2-0 victory and it was reported as such in publications in both Hull and Leicester. In the final Second Division table published on April 28, 1913, City's record was given as: goals scored 60, goals conceded 55. Leicester's tally was registered as: goals scored 49, goals conceded 65. Yet in subsequent record-books and indeed the Football League's own records the game is recorded as a 2-1 win to the Tigers. And their overall record is: goals scored 60, goals conceded 56. Leicester's final record is: goals scored 50, goals conceded 65. The mysterious amendment did not alter any League positions, but it is a perfect explanation as to why City fans must have felt depressingly fated about the club's fortunes from the early years.

The next instance occurred in the second round of the FA Cup on November 26, 1960, and had remarkable repercussions. The Tigers had beaten non-League Sutton Town 3-0 at Boothferry Park in the first round and were then drawn away to Darlington. Dudley Price gave City a 1-0 lead at Feethams and they were hanging on to it when a controversial incident occurred in the final minute. The Quakers' left-winger Bobby Baxter crossed the ball from the left and City goalkeeper Bernard Fisher was convinced that it had dropped over the bar when referee Jim Parkinson signalled a goal. Fisher had spontaneously gone behind his goal to retrieve the ball, but Mr Parkinson consulted a linesman and it was decided that it had gone under the bar and then through a hole in the net. There again Baxter was not immediately congratulated by his teammates for scoring such an important, face-saving goal.

Fisher insisted, though, that there was no hole in the net and he said:"When the cross came over, I followed it and jumped up with it. The ball definitely went over. In fact, my finger-tips touched the bar as the ball went over. I went round the back of the net to pick up the ball and when the cheer went up, I thought it was for time. Then I heard the shouts of 'Goal!' and I was flabber-gasted. I just could not believe it. The ball landed on the roof of the net, ran along it to the support at the side and then ran down the back of the net more or less in the middle."

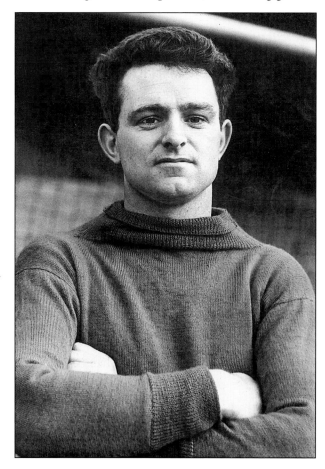

Hull City goalkeeper Bernard Fisher, who was at the centre of the FA Cup controversy at Darlington in 1960.

Mr Parkinson was surrounded by angry City players and coach Gus McLean had to intercede. But the goal had to stand, it was a 1-1 draw and a replay was necessary. Yet the saga, in fact, was just beginning. Two days later there was another 1-1 draw at Boothferry Park when Chris Chilton was on the mark for the Tigers in front of an 18,125 crowd. Extra time was needed, so there were already 210 minutes on the clock. The action then switched to a neutral ground – Elland Road, Leeds – on December 5 when there was another 1-1 draw and Price was again City's marksman. But there was no extra time on this occasion because the pitch was such a quagmire that the tie was abandoned at the end of the 90 minutes. A week later the two sides met again and this time the venue was Doncaster Rovers' Belle Vue Ground. On this occasion it did not finish 1-1: it was 0-0 and there was extra time and there would have to be a fourth replay. Three days later the two sides trooped off to Middlesbrough's Ayresome Park and the Tigers, in particular, were probably getting a bit fed up by it all by then, so they emphatically settled it once and for all after 510 minutes and a dubious goal that started it all off. The biggest crowd of the series – 19,366 – watched it and City won 3-0 with goals by Doug Clarke, Ralph Gubbins and Dave King, who was making his first appearance in the saga.

City must have then wondered whether it really was worth all the trouble because they lost 1-0 at home to Gubbins' old club Bolton Wanderers, who had also knocked them out of the inaugural Football League Cup earlier in the season, in the third round. But was it all the more exciting and dramatic because of the constant replays and the original necessity for them instead of resorting fairly quickly to a penalty shoot-out, as is now the custom? Or would it have been a lot more clear-cut if Mr Parkinson had been able to consult a TV eye to clarify his thoughts rather than just a linesman?

Hull City's Doug Clarke takes on Swindon Town's long-serving defender John Trollope in the controversial game between the two sides at Boothferry Park in May 1963.

One crazy aspect of it all was that history then basically repeated itself at Boothferry Park on May 18, 1963, when City entertained Swindon Town in a Third Division game in front of 4,361 fans. There was a not a lot at stake in what was an end-of-season affair because the Tigers were ensconced in mid-table and Town were already promoted, but it was just as well that they were. It finished 1-1 after John McSeveney had equalised for City after 53 minutes, but the controversy stemmed from what had gone on before. Swindon were awarded the lead after 23 minutes when a shot by Ernie Hunt lodged at the bottom of one of the back stanchions of the goal and City goalkeeper Mike Williams went round the outside to retrieve the ball for a goal-kick. But referee Windle signalled a goal after consulting a linesman, believing that the shot had gone inside the post and then through some loose rigging at the back of the net before coming to rest outside it. Swindon's players made no initial move to congratulate Hunt for scoring and the decision instigated a long delay while City players protested ardently to Mr Windle, who was later involved in two scuffles in the tunnel in which the police had to intervene. But the so-called goal stood and City's players missed out on their £2-per-man win bonuses!

Almost nine years later the Tigers again came across Hunt in an FA Cup tie at Coventry, with whom he featured in another controversy after he had scored following a new style of free-kick in which the ball was flicked up for him to volley, and he cryptically said beforehand: "I have happy memories of Hull!" But the irony of the clash with Swindon was that City fans had already been upset earlier in the season when the first meeting in that particularly raw winter had been abandoned at halftime because the Boothferry Park pitch had become too icy.

And it was during the bad weather of the winter of the 1962-63 season that City went on an FA Cup marathon of a different kind. They beat non-League Crook Town 5-4 at home in the first round and then defeated Workington 2-0, also at Boothferry Park. That earned them a visit to First Division strugglers Leyton Orient in the third round and the tie eventually took place at Brisbane Road on February 11, 1963 – at the ninth time of asking. The bad weather had ensured that it had previously been postponed on January 5, 8, 15, 21, 26 and 30 and February 4 and 6. When the tie finally went ahead, City, then in the Third Division, bravely defied the odds and it was drawn 1-1 with the ramifications of having to fit in a replay. That was postponed just once – on February 13 because Boothferry Park was covered in ice and snow. But it took place six days later – and promptly went into extra time before Orient won 2-0. And such was the severity of that winter that City completed only those two cup ties between December 29 and March 4. The concept of the mid-season break, therefore, may not be entirely new…

And if there were goals and games that never were, there was also technically a City player who never was. He did exist and he did sign for the club – but he never played for them. He was Bill Wright, who joined the Tigers in August 1961 from Plymouth Argyle after spells with his home-town club Blackpool, Leicester City and Newcastle United. City agreed a fee with the Pilgrims and made arrangements to find accommodation for Wright, but ten days later he changed his mind. Wright was described as a utility forward, but he decided that he wanted to be a left-winger with the Tigers and nothing else. But City manager Cliff Britton would make no guar-

Ground staff at Boothferry Park make sure that the pitch is finally fit for Hull City's FA Cup replay with Leyton Orient in February 1963. Referee Ken Stokes (left) and City manager Cliff Britton watch the work being carried out.

antees to him, so he at once agreed to Wright's plea to be released from his contract. No transfer fee was paid and Wright would probably be regarded as something of a trendsetter because he would surely record at least eight on the world-famous combined Unsworth-van Hooijdonk-Collymore-Anelka scale nowadays!

The Tigers did have one far more genuine soccer trendsetter, goalkeeper Tony Norman. It happened when City beat Wimbledon 1-0 at Boothferry Park on September 27, 1983, with a goal by Billy Whitehurst and Norman used the game to develop a way of kicking the ball differently. Traditionally, goalkeepers would distribute the ball by either drop-kicking or punting it from the hand or throwing or rolling it out to a teammate. In this instance Norman began to throw the ball down in front of him – often a few feet outside the penalty area – and then kick it from the ground as a deliberate tactical manoeuvre. Dave Bassett, then Wimbledon's manager, duly noted the tactic and instructed his own goalkeeper Dave Beasant to use it equally as regularly for their famed long-ball game of the time. Other goalkeepers gradually caught on to the idea and bit by bit the ploy became custom and practice in the game.

There was a suggestion that the seeds had been sown on an isolated basis in a game involving the Tigers at Gillingham, whose goalkeeper Ron Hillyard had been forced to kick that way because of the combination of a strong wind and an injury handicap. But Norman said:"I might have seen someone else do it, but I honestly don't know where I got the idea from. I don't know why I started to do it other than the fact that it was good for the way that we wanted to play at the time. We didn't have the biggest players up front on some occasions, so I thought it was easier to roll the ball out and then drill it anyway. It meant that the kick looped in the air if you drilled it and the front players could hold it up a bit better. And I found after I'd done it that it was more accurate anyway. Dave Beasant has acknowledged that he started to do it at Wimbledon after he'd seen me do it and in the end everybody started doing it."

Norman, in fact, was always liable to do something a bit different at the best of times. After all, he used to kick the ball right-footed and yet throw it out with his left arm. As a cricketer, he is a right-handed batsman and a left-arm bowler. And he plays golf right-handed, but writes left-handed…

The Tigers had set another soccer trend as a club on January 6, 1951, when they met Everton in the FA Cup at Boothferry Park. City became the first club to have their own railway station adjoining their ground because that was the day on which Boothferry Park Halt was opened behind the East Stand. The service ferried fans on an eight-minute trip from Hull's Paragon Station to the ground and six trains carried both City and Everton fans on that inaugural journey. There was also a return journey at the end of the game, but the first eight-coach train, pulled by loco-motive number 61080, left Paragon Station with 595 supporters on board at 12.54 that afternoon and the others followed at ten-minute intervals. Four sets of stock were used, the first two returning to Paragon Station for second trips. The non-corridor stock, in fact, had been sent from King's Cross in London, where it had been used on suburban lines, and the blind in the indicator above the guard's compartment on the first train still showed Potters Bar. It is not thought, however, that any Arsenal fans were still on it!

The service regularly operated for much smaller crowds over the years, but, like the steam engines on that first afternoon, it eventually became redundant. And it was not unknown for disgruntled fans to leave before the end if City were losing, make a dash to be first on the train and then watch the last rites of the game from the comparative luxury of their own railway compartment before getting away from it all as quickly as they could. And when locomotives or trains do still occasionally travel past Boothferry Park during a game, it has been common for the engine-drivers to hoot something appropriate to the participants while shuttling by. Curiously enough, City's previous ground at Anlaby Road had been close to two railway lines in and out of Paragon Station and when junior games were no longer staged there from the 1960s, it was because an extra spur was to be constructed between them both – and the railroad went through the middle of the ground…

But City have also found to their cost that change does not always work out well for them. Their colours, for example, have traditionally been amber and black, as might naturally befit a team called the Tigers. Sometimes the shirts have been plain amber and something they have had amber-and-black stripes. The designs have frequently changed, most notably in 1964-65 when their shirts had two black hoops and their shorts were yellow and certainly not amber. The fans, in fact, dubbed it the custard-pie look and it did not last long.

But City had a drastic colour change to blue and white for the start of the 1935-36 season. The new strip was not unveiled until the opening League game of the season at home to Fulham on August 31, 1935, when it was reported: "City turned out in the club's new colours of ultra-marine shirts with white collars and cuffs. They wore white knickers and blue-and-white striped hose. On the breast of the shirt are the coat-of-arms of Hull – three crowns – and the whole attire presented a smart appearance." The game ended in a 1-1 draw, but the new look did not do much for City's fortunes because they were relegated that season after finishing at the bottom of the Second Division. They no longer looked like Tigers and it would seem that they did not play too much like them, either. The amber and black soon returned.

Yet in 1946 there was a new regime in charge and they wanted to break with the past. New chairman Harold Needler had wanted to form a new professional soccer club in Hull, but even though he could not do so, it did not prevent him and his colleagues from trying to erase some of the memories and traditions of the past. That included the team's colours, so they came up with orange shirts, which bore the civic crest of three crowns, white shorts and orange socks, all of which had blue trimmings, but the Board of Trade would not release the necessary dyes for them. The alternative was a strip of pale blue shirts and white shorts although the old amber-and-black colours were occasionally utilised, but at the end of the 1946-47 season the experiment was abandoned and it was back to amber shirts with a tiger logo and black shorts.

This time, fortunately, the colour change had not brought relegation, but there are plenty of instances when ill-luck has descended on City. They must, for example, be one of the few clubs ever to have had a player sent off because of the nails in one of his boots! It happened in a Second Division game that ended in a 1-1 draw at Middlesbrough on the evening of September 12, 1928. George Camsell scored for 'Boro' and Ken McDonald was on the mark for City, but both sides were disrupted by injuries. The Tigers were handicapped when Arthur Prince suffered a twisted knee and McDonald received a nasty kick on the ankle, while 'Boro' were without John Peacock's services for 15 minutes and Jack Carr had his shirt torn after getting a kick in the chest. But the major controversy surrounded City centre-half Arthur Childs, who was later to be sent off in the club's only appearance in the FA Cup semi-finals. Ten minutes from the end Childs tackled Middlesbrough's winger Billy Millar, who received a gashed arm in the challenge. Referee Hull then examined Childs' boots and ordered him to the dressing-room to have a nail removed. Childs dashed back on to the pitch in a different pair of boots shortly afterwards, but Mr Hull sent him off again. It was reported: "The referee was strictly in his rights in taking this action. Law 12 of the game, which deals with the kind of foot-gear permitted, lays down clearly that any player infringing the law shall be prohibited from taking further part in the match." It was accepted that the incident was accidental, but Mr Hull later admitted that Childs' dismissal was "for wearing boots with protruding nails." City's only saving grace was that he would not receive a suspension for his sending-off.

Such incidents have made life tough for the Tigers' fans in general, but the club can at least count on some loyal and stoical support from a number of well-known celebrities. Thankfully there has never quite been the same show-business brouhaha with sundry hangers-on that has often been the case at the big clubs. City's celebrity followers do not go to football in the remotest kind of ostentatious manner: they go to games as quietly and anonymously as possible and they genuinely love their club, who are, in turn, fortunate to have them at their core of support. Following a club such as the Tigers is a serious business that can have a severe effect on the emotions and requires the utmost dedication and gravitas as well as nerves of steel. And there are noteworthy figures who have unstintingly given their all with a ready willingness to support good causes at the drop of a hat if they have anything to do with City.

Leading actor Tom Courtenay is one of those personalities who has followed City's fortunes closely wherever his travels have taken him. In fact, it was Tom who introduced fellow actor Omar Sharif to the delights of City while they were filming *Dr Zhivago* n Paris together. Tom would regularly send out messengers from the set to ring the old Hull City score service to find out how the Tigers had fared and it seems that eventually Omar Sharif became equally interested in finding out the results! The story is on a par with one concerning former City and Republic of Ireland goalkeeper Maurice Swan, one of the heroes of

Actor Tom Courtenay with his Dalmatian dog Wagstaff, named after Hull City favourite Ken Wagstaff.

their 1965-66 promotion campaign. He is a close friend of Irish premier Bertie Ahern, who has now apparently been programmed into avidly looking for the Tigers' results amid the complexities of going about his political business!

And I have an enduring memory of a social evening in London when all Tom wanted was to find out more from manager Stan Ternent about some of the Tigers' promising youngsters whom he had just met. But he was sidetracked by Ternent's impressive knowledge of some of his acting credits and his great interest in them. I think they called it a draw!

Tom has been so dedicated to City that he did, in fact, once own an impressive spotted dog which he called "Wagstaff" after Ken Wagstaff. On one trip to Hull he apparently took Wagstaff the dog into the home dressing-room at Boothferry Park to meet the Wagstaff the player. The two Wagstaffs were sitting next to each other when goalkeeper Ian McKechnie is understood to have observed: "The dog's better looking, but Ken's got more spots!"

Such matters can also be confusing because there was also a racehorse called "Waggy" in the 1960s. That in itself is a little misleading because there was also a horse called Hull City, which ran in six races in Ireland in 1967 and never won. And it was in 1963 that an Irish club, Bangor, asked the Tigers if they wanted to buy them for £9,000 and adopt them as a nursery side. It never happened, presumably because of the loneliness of the long-distance takeover…

Playwright Alan Plater, actor Roy North, actor-manager Barrie Rutter and film director Mark Herman have also retained a close interest in the Tigers' fortunes. At

Leading playwright and Hull City buff Alan Plater.

times this has even been known to include references to City in their work on suitable occasions. Alan explained: "If my work from the last 35 years were to come under close scrutiny, then I think people would find that I use characters' names as an opportunity to make oblique references to my heroes, who are normally footballers or jazz musicians. The boring way to come up with characters' names is to go through a telephone book: the best way is to name characters after people you like. It goes without saying, therefore, that the name Carter has appeared more than once in things I've written over the years!"

Alan will also pen a few lines or say a few words on behalf of any cause to do with City and yet he was even banished from the southern supporters' club's membership list by Martin Fish for backing me when I was banned from covering the club's matches by the chairman. Alan

Actor Roy North is given a lesson in pitch maintenance at Boothferry Park by Hull City's John Davies (left) and Stan McEwan in 1986.

equalised with his 1998 stage play called *All Credit to the Lads*, whose plot included two banned soccer writers! The play also includes a classic explanation of what he feels should be the origins of true fans' allegiances on the lines of: "Football teams are like parents – you are born with them and you don't have any choice about them…"

Roy North, who sprung to fame as Basil Brush's companion, once assembled a showbiz team, who included Sheffield Wednesday striker Scott Oakes' father Trevor, from Showaddywaddy, to play in a testimonial game in Hull, but was then unable to fulfil his dream of playing at Boothferry Park when he had to drop out with a serious knee injury. It is probably not surprising then that he has remained a close friend of former City physiotherapist Jeff Radcliffe.

In recent years Barrie Rutter has run his own theatre company called *Northern Broadside*. The story goes that the company were appearing at a London venue when he found out that the Tigers were playing in the area at the same time. Apparently the whole company were told that it would be compulsory for them to watch City's match as a prelude to their performance in their play that night!

Mark Herman, the mastermind behind hit films such as *Brassed Off* and *Little Voice*, was once disappointed that he was unable to attend a tribute dinner to City winger Ian Butler because he was attending Robert Redford's Sundance Film Festival in America. He made up for it for by donating a raffle prize for the function and sending a message on the lines of: "You've never really been a Robert Redford to look at, Ian, but there again he could never go past full-backs as if they weren't there!"

Mark also co-wrote the club song *The Tigers Are Back*, their anthem as they emerged from the depression of receivership in 1982, with fellow supporter Henry Priestman, who went on to enjoy regular chart success as the keyboards player with the Christians. And on another musical note, Paul Denman, the bass player with Sade, is also a staunch City fan. He once made what might almost be the ultimate sacrifice of donating one of the band's gold discs for a fund-raising cause connected with the club.

Then there is the example of popular TV actor Tim Healy, who has starred in *Auf Wiedersehen, Pet, Boys from the Bush* and *Heartburn Hotel*. In a 1999 TV play he was the manager of a fictitious team

Top film director Mark Herman in his Hull City scarf.

called Bostock Stanley, who were deemed to have beaten Hull City on their way to the FA Cup Final. It must have been tough for him to play the part for one very good reason – his grandfather William Clark made one appearance for the Tigers as a left-winger in a 1-0 home defeat against Blackpool on March 20, 1920. It just goes to prove that nothing ever comes easily or logically for anyone who has any kind of interest to declare in Hull City…

Chapter Three

Take That!

HULL City may never achieve their ultimate ambition of playing in top-flight English soccer, but they have still proved at times that they can match the best in the land. The reason that they have constantly flattered to deceive is that they have simply not consistently done well enough in League football. Many of their greatest achievements have been in one-off instances in cup ties instead and in their history they have claimed the scalps of some of the biggest names in English club football, many of them who are currently in the FA Premiership.

In their formative years in the early part of the 20th century City were not involved in either promotion or relegation, but they made a name for themselves as frequent giantkillers in the FA Cup. They regularly caused upsets and their reputation grew nationally as a result of some of their one-off feats in which they ruffled the feathers of English soccer's status quo.

It all started in the 1907-08 season when they disposed of Woolwich Arsenal, as they were then called. They did not become known as Arsenal until they were relegated from the old First Division in the 1912-13 season, but the Tigers provided them with something else that they probably wanted to forget in those days when they knocked them out of the FA Cup at the first-round stage. Arsenal were having a moderate season in the First Division and eventually finished in the lower half of the table as the joint fifth of six sides who all finished on the same number of points. But they were given a home tie against the Tigers on January 11, 1908.

City prepared for the game at Plumstead by taking a break in Worthing although skipper Gordon Wright did not join the party until later in the week. They used training facilities provided by the local club in Worthing and the preparations included a three-mile walk along the seafront and a visit to the town's Theatre Royal to see a performance of *The Earl and The Girl*. The Tigers then moved on to London's Manchester Hotel nearer the game, for which centre-half William Robinson was passed fit after struggling throughout the week with a shoulder injury, while Frank Martin was preferred in attack to Joe Shaw.

City were forced to defend stoutly at times and Arsenal did hit the woodwork on one occasion in the first half, but they could not beat the heroic Martin Spendiff in goal and it was reported: "Shots were rained in at him, but he treated them all alike and, by his cool, clever and resourceful methods, he gained great admiration from almost every one of the 35,000 appreciative audience." Most of City's threats came from winger Joe "Stanley" Smith, but Arthur Temple and Martin wasted their best chances. The Tigers had left-half Davy Gordon injured in the last minute, but they hung on for a goalless draw and Arsenal's directors sarcastically suggested afterwards that they would offer "a sovereign apiece to all our players who can score in an open goal!"

It was agreed between the two sets of directors that the replay was to take place at Anlaby Road five days later, but Gordon missed it and the rest of the season because of a broken collarbone, so Shaw significantly returned to the side. The winners knew that there was a second-round trip to Aston Villa at stake and there was plenty of interest in the tie in Hull. Many firms closed so that their workers could watch the tie although it was rumoured that elsewhere on the day "the mortality rate among aged relatives, mothers-in-law and aunts had gone up tremendously during the morning, judging by the young men in offices who wanted to attend burials in the afternoon!" City were based at Withernsea's Queen's Hotel during the build-up to the replay, but accommodation in Hull was scarce because of a Labour convention, so the Arsenal party travelled by train from King's Cross and stayed overnight in Doncaster before the tie.

The crowd of about 15,000 soon went into raptures when the Tigers, who had the wind at their backs, took the lead in only the ninth minute. Gordon Wright sped down the line and Joe Shaw took his pass in his stride to score with a powerful drive.

Both players were schoolteachers at various times: on this occasion it was the start of Arsenal being given a soccer lesson because there was no stopping rampant City. Wright created a second chance with his pace and whipped in a centre as Jack Smith and Shaw moved in. Shaw supplied the finish to make it 2-0 and after 20 minutes Arthur Temple added a third goal when he scored at the second attempt after the ball had rebounded to him off the bar. That

Hull City's Browell brothers (left to right): Anthony, George and Tom.

was how it stayed until halftime although City were handicapped when George "Tot" Hedley hurt his knee after colliding with his own player, George Browell, and had to go on to the wing. He limped off at one stage, but returned in the second half when the tempo of the game began to subside. The Tigers, though, soon made it 4-0 when Joe Smith paved the way for Jack Smith to score from close range. Goalkeeper Martin Spendiff needed attention, but seemed dazed when he resumed and near the end Arsenal managed a consolation goal when a corner was not properly cleared and Peter Kyle ran through to score from close range. Frank Martin was the next City player to be injured and there was plenty of laughter among the ecstatic crowd when one of the galoshes belonging to the doctor treating him dropped off in the commotion!

The stunning 4-1 triumph resulted in many fans gathering in front of the stand to cheer their heroes, while the receipts of £572 and the prospect of a lucrative trip to Aston Villa meant that the club had a chance to pay up all their liabilities. But in the second round City went out 3-0 at Villa, who were on their way to becoming the First Division's runners-up behind Manchester United.

The Tigers' next giantkilling act took place in the 1910-11 season and was a singular act of vengeance. The previous season they had been pipped for a place in the First Division on goal average by Oldham Athletic. City, who had been knocked out of the FA Cup by Chelsea in the previous two seasons, beat Bristol Rovers in the first round, drawing 0-0 away on January 14, 1911, and winning the replay 1-0 after extra time with a goal by defender Jack McQuillan five days later. That earned the Tigers a home tie against Oldham, who had adapted well to life in the First Division, on February 4, 1911. A twist of fate meant that the chance for revenge over the Latics had arrived more quickly then might have been expected.

City were based at the Queen's Hotel in Withernsea for their preparations, which included long walks and salt-water baths, but their build-up did not go entirely smoothly. During a light-hearted round of golf at the local Withernsea club, during which "the powers-that-be at St. Andrew's would have held up their hands in horror to see their rules so frequently broken," manager Ambrose Langley was injured by a stray ball. And then there was the threat of a train strike, so emergency plans were discussed for the City party to return to Hull from the coast by taxis if necessary. As it was, the Tigers made two changes for the tie, bringing in Joe "Stanley" Smith and Tom "Boy" Browell for Frank Martin and Vinny Townend. Oldham also prepared for the game on the east coast – at Bridlington.

Former City centre-forward Alf Toward was in Oldham's side, but during the first half he twisted awkwardly as he fell and aggravated an old injury. The Tigers, for their part, also had an injury setback because William "Tim" Wright was knocked out at one point and ended up as something of a passenger on the wing. Tom Browell was also in the wars himself when he received a kick in the face, but that did not prevent him from playing a part in the only goal of the game that sent sections of the 17,500 crowd swaying "like a field of corn swept by the wind." City welcomed the greasy surface at Anlaby Road after the midweek frost, but it almost cost them their goal. Wally Smith cleverly got himself into a position to deliver a cross, but Browell slipped as he prepared to shoot. Fortunately, the ball ran clear to the Tigers' ace marksman, Arthur Temple, who coolly placed it in the back of the net. It was enough to see City through and the players each received a bonus of £5 for their efforts.

The Tigers then went out of the FA Cup in the third round when they lost 3-2 at First Division Newcastle United despite two goals from Joe Smith. Oldham, meanwhile, sent City out of the FA Cup in the first round in 1911-12 to exact their own retribution.

City next turned their giant-killing attention to West Bromwich Albion, then a mid-table First Division outfit, during the 1914-15 campaign. They met on January 9, 1915, in the first round. It was a plum draw for the Tigers because Albion had won the trophy twice and been the beaten Finalists on four other occasions. And five of their side who faced City had played in the 1911-12 Final when they lost 1-0 to Barnsley in a replay. In contrast, City's right-winger David Mercer was making his FA Cup debut and centre-half Charles Deacey was facing his old club. The Tigers were forced to make one change in defence, Douglas Morgan taking over from John Pattison, who had been injured in the 3-0 defeat at Stockport County in the League on New Year's Day.

Deacey was at his best against his old club, but City's centre-forward Sammy Stevens, who originally came from Staffordshire, also had a point to prove because Albion had once signed him and then not even given him a trial match. The Tigers had hoped that referee Howcroft would give him plenty of protection because he had come in for some harsh treatment in recent games: he did do and Stevens retaliated against the Throstles by scoring the only goal of the game. City's forward-line, though, were a little disjointed because William "Kilty" Cameron had to struggle on after receiving two nasty kicks. But the Tigers' big hero was goalkeeper Nicholson Hendry, who produced a series of magnificent saves. And on the only occasion on which Hendry was beaten, Joe Edelston, whose son Maurice was to become a noted soccer commentator, came to his rescue with a vital clearance in a tie that kept the 13,000 crowd on tenterhooks.

The Tigers' directors treated the players to a celebration dinner at the city's Grosvenor Hotel after the game and thanked them for their help "during a most trying period." Skipper Billy Halligan made only a short speech in reply, insisting that he was saving himself for when he received the FA Cup!

City beat Northampton Town 2-1 at home with two more goals by Sammy Stevens in the second round and then beat Southampton at the second attempt, drawing 2-2 away after extra time and then winning the replay 4-0 with two more goals from Stevens, but then they controversially went down 4-2 to Bolton Wanderers in the quarter-finals.

Soon after World War One, City were up to their giantkilling exploits again and it was a remarkable feat all-round. In the 1920-21 season the Tigers had beaten Bath City 3-0 at home and then Crystal Palace 2-0 away in the opening two rounds of the FA Cup. They were then drawn at home to Burnley, who were on their way to winning the First Division title with five points to spare over Manchester City. When the Tigers met them in the third round on February 19, 1921, they were on their way to a record 30 League matches without defeat. City were having an average season in the Second Division, but it was to turn out to be a classic tale of the unexpected.

Hull City's Scottish centre-half Mick Gilhooley.

Burnley were not at full strength because the influential George Halley had pneumonia and prolific goalscorer Joe Anderson was also missing, but they were still able to field a side including some of the players who had helped them to beat Liverpool 1-0 in the last FA Cup Final to be held at Crystal Palace in 1913-14. Anderson's place, in fact, was taken by Ben Freeman, who had been the scorer of Burnley's winner that day. City had gone 13 League games without a win earlier in the season: at this point they were stuck in a run of another ten without a victory, so an upset seemed unlikely. But they strengthened their half-back line with return of Mick "Rubberneck" Gilhooley and Tommy Bleakley, while Irishman Harry Wilson was back on the left-wing in place of James Marshall, who had just played his only game on trial for the club.

City were confident of causing a major shock as they had a light lunch at the city's Grosvenor Hotel and they were spurred on by a crowd of 26,000. Gilhooley bottled up Anderson and the Tigers, who had prepared for the tie at Ravenscar, never relented as a side, gradually knocking Burnley out of their stride. In fact, it was reported that "the Burnley machine was clogged at every turn" and a minute before halftime City took the lead. Burnley left-back Cliff Jones conceded a free-kick, John Collier took it and Harry Sargeaunt had a drive blocked from it. But inside-right Tommy Brandon, who had regularly played in defence until David Mercer's departure to Sheffield United, reacted first to head past England international goalkeeper Jerry Dawson. After 62 minutes Brandon scored his second goal with a spectacular 30-yard drive and 14 minutes from time Wilson sealed an amazing 3-0 victory when he took his toll of some hesitant Burnley defending to nip in for a third goal.

The stunning success was described as City's "greatest victory of all" and gave chairman Jim Spring a particularly happy birthday: he probably thought that all his birthdays had come at once that day! The Tigers met more First Division opposition, Preston North End, in the quarter-finals, but lost 1-0 in a replay after drawing 0-0 at home.

The following season City were at it again in the FA Cup when they were drawn at home to First Division Middlesbrough in the first round on January 7, 1922. The win over Burnley had been emphatic, but this time they recorded their biggest victory to date over a fellow League side in the competition. The Tigers were hit by injuries as they prepared for the tie at Ilkley and there were rumours that the club were about to sell skipper Mick Gilhooley to Burnley after he had done so well against them the previous season. But City officials insisted that the club were buoyant financially, pointing out that the prospect of a big gate against Middlesbrough meant that it was planned to clear their bank overdraft and pay the accounts from their own money for the first time in their existence! 'Boro,' meanwhile, had just lost 6-1 to Sheffield United in the League when their Scottish international centre-forward Andrew Wilson had to play even though he was unfit because George Elliott had missed his train! But they welcomed back another Scottish international, John Marshall, after a four-week suspension.

The game attracted a 23,000 attendance and City outsmarted Middlesbrough throughout, repeatedly hitting the woodwork before Jackie Crawford, who had been giving left-back Victor Fox a harrowing afternoon, gave them the lead with a well-worked goal after 38 minutes. It was one-way traffic after the interval as the creative Bob Coverdale made it 2-0 after 53 minutes and the hard-working Bert "Paddy" Mills added a third 11 minutes later. And in the last five minutes City completed a 5-0 rout when Tommy Bleakley scored the goal that he had deserved and Coverdale added his second with a chip. It was back to the city's Grosvenor Hotel again for another celebratory dinner that night.

In the fourth round City lost 3-0 at Nottingham Forest, who were on their way to the Second Division title, but there was another noteworthy postscript to the big win over Middlesbrough. Gilhooley had had another outstanding day against Andrew Wilson and a month later he was capped by Scotland against Wales. But a month after that City did what they were repeatedly to do throughout their history – they sold one of their best players. And it was Gilhooley who went, after all, joining First Division Sunderland for what was briefly a British record fee of £5,250.

In the 1926-27 season City produced a double act of giantkilling in the FA Cup for the first time because they knocked out two First Division sides in the same season. The Tigers were doing reasonably well in the Second Division, but their victims, West Bromwich Albion and then Everton, were fighting to avoid the drop into it. As it was, Albion finished bottom and went down, while Everton survived even though they finished only two places higher and the following season they were the League champions.

City were drawn at home to West Bromwich in the third round on January 8, 1927, and prepared for the tie with a ten-day break on the coast, stopping off to make Bridlington's Alexandra Hotel their base after they had lost 3-1 at South Shields on New Year's Day. And recent signing George Guyan, their goalscorer in that game against his old club, was replaced at centre-forward by William Cowan for the cup tie. Cowan had scored a hat-trick at Darlington in the League earlier in the season and made the case for his recall with another one in the reserves against Halifax Town. The fans wanted him back in the side and it was even suggested that he was being given unfair treatment because City had been fined after an irregularity surrounding his transfer to them from Gateshead side High Fell. Albion, who warmed up for the game at Hornsea, had a poor defensive record, but they welcomed back their England international right-back William Ashurst.

Wet weather restricted the attendance to 18,000 and left the Anlaby Road pitch as a quagmire, but the Tigers got off to a great start when the recalled Cowan scored from Henry Scott's pass in the the fourth minute. But City were handicapped when Tommy Bleakley dislocated his knee and eventually had to change positions with George Whitworth. With 25 minutes left Nelson Howarth headed home a free-kick conceded by Stan Dixon to make it 1-1 and Albion had a great chance to take the lead, but in the 70th minute the Tigers scored the winner following a free-kick of their own. Bleakley touched it to left-winger William Taylor, who set up the chance for Scott to drill home a superb goal with a fierce left-foot drive to seal a 2-1 victory in fading light.

The first fourth-round meeting with Everton took place on January 29, 1927, at Anlaby Road, but although George Martin passed a fitness test, City were without the injured Tommy Bleakley, so Cornelius Sullivan took his place with Christopher Swan continuing in the other wing-half berth. Neither George Guyan nor William Cowan played this time with Alfred Horne retaining his place in the forward-line instead. Everton, who had previously played a friendly in Hull in October 1912 as part of the transfer deal when Anthony Browell, Tom Browell and Joe Smith left City, booked into Bridlington's Britannia Hotel towards the end of their preparations and included 20-year-old England centre-forward William "Dixie" Dean although they were involved in transfer talks with Sunderland to try to sign two other internationals, Warneford Cresswell and Robert Kelly. The Tigers had also prepared for the tie at Bridlington.

The Tigers had the fillip of taking the lead after just 15 minutes with an excellent goal by Martin after George Whitworth and William Taylor had created the opening, but then they wasted their chances. Dean was well policed by City captain Matt Bell, but he also had an off-day in front of goal and it was not until 20 minutes from time that Everton drew level. Albert Virr scored with a shot that left City goalkeeper George "Geordie" Maddison unsighted and the Toffeemen finished the stronger to the disappointment of most of the 22,000 crowd.

Four days later the action switched to Goodison Park for the replay with City staying at Blackpool's Carlton Hotel in-between. The Tigers had doubts about Bell, who had been injured in the 1-1 draw at Anlaby Road, and George Maddison and Stan Dixon because of illness, but all three played and they made only two changes. In the forward-line Horne and Whitworth were replaced by Guyan and George McLaughlin. Everton, who tried out brine baths during their build-up, also made two changes. The winners, in the meantime, knew that they would go to Wolverhampton Wanderers in the fourth round.

The crowd of 45,000 saw Everton take the lead after just four minutes when their Scottish international winger Alex Troup beat City's offside trap and it might have been worse if Maddison had not been on top form. But in the 40th minute he was beaten by a first-time shot from "Dixie" Dean as Everton led 2-0 at the break. Eight minutes into the second half, though, City reduced the arrears when George Martin cleverly set up the chance for Henry Scott to score with a low drive. The inspirational Martin was also the architect of the Tigers' equaliser 20 minutes from the end when he centred for Guyan to score from five yards out. It forced extra time, but the score at 2-2 although City had a let-off when Everton were denied a penalty after John McGee had appeared to handle.

A coin was tossed for the choice of venue for the second replay five days later and Everton won it, opting for some obscure geographical reason to take the sides to Villa Park, Birmingham, where the game was watched by a crowd of 16,800. City brought back Whitworth in place of McLaughlin, while Everton made three changes although Dean was in their line-up after he had pulled out of an England trial match at Bolton.

The Tigers led after just eight minutes when Whitworth set up the chance for Guyan to score an opportunist goal, but Dean cleverly lobbed home Everton's equaliser in the 21st minute. City, though, were back in front after 41 minutes when Whitworth scored with a momentous solo effort after bursting through from the halfway line. But then the two City goalscorers were injured: almost immediately Whitworth had to go off with a suspected broken nose although he returned to play on the wing after the break, while Guyan was left limping after a collision. The Tigers, though, held out until 30 seconds from the end when Arthur Dominy scored Everton's second equaliser and extra time was again needed. But in the 100th minute City took the lead for the third time in the match and it was enough to see them through. Martin crashed the ball home from Guyan's corner – and then the uproar began because it had burst. Everton's players claimed that the goal was invalid because of the deflated ball, but City's captain Matt Bell pointed out that it had bounced after going over the line and referee Musther allowed it to stand.

City's 3-2 win was watched by Wolverhampton Wanderers' players, but their cup hopes were dashed in typically-disappointing circumstances in the fifth round. They went down 1-0 away to Wolves, who were to finish eight places below them in the Second Division.

Three seasons later City were to reach the FA Cup semi-finals for the only time in their history and they came up with another giantkilling double along the way. Their run began with a 4-3 win at Plymouth Argyle, in which Stan Alexander hit a hat-trick, and then a 3-1 victory at Anlaby Road against Blackpool, to whom they would lose 3-0 in a home League game designated as a benefit occasion for Matt Bell, Tommy Bleakley and George Maddison later in the season. But then the Tigers' run gained impetus as they disposed of Manchester City, who were to finish third in the First Division that season, and Newcastle United, who were to end up avoiding relegation to the Second Division by one point.

City visited Manchester City at Maine Road in the fifth round on February 15, 1930, and suffered a setback before the game had started when Matt Bell failed a fitness test on his injured ankle. His ready-made replacement, Gordon Wilson, was missing with a thigh strain and it was decided not to risk Arthur Rodgers again, so Scottish international Jimmy Howieson took his place at left-back. The Tigers visited their local electric and vapour baths during their build-up, while the

Manchester City players settled for a golf trip to the Northenden links course. Their injury problems were clearing up and they had a final boost when their skipper Jimmy McMullan, the Scottish international, was fit to return.

The tie attracted a 61,574 crowd, but the Tigers were forced to play into the wind in the first half and, as they struggled to adjust to the slippery surface, they went behind in the fourth minute when Ernie Toseland scored after Bobby Marshall had created the opportunity. But the equaliser came after 29 minutes when Billy Taylor raced past McMullan and Billy Felton and set up the chance for Bert "Paddy" Mills to head home. Then the Tigers fashioned a second goal after 64 minutes when the dangerous Stan Alexander sped away from McMullan and crossed for Taylor, making up for his disappointment when he had been Cardiff City's 12th man at the same ground in the quarter-finals in 1923-24, scored with a spinning shot and it finished 2-1.

City goalkeeper Fred Gibson, who had been in defiant mood, was chaired from the field by a group of supporters and Matt Bell was not too distraught when he was struck by a missile while watching the game from the stands. The Tigers had reached the quarter-finals by beating the leading sides in three different divisions at the time and a visit to Newcastle, where there was to be an even bigger crowd of 63,486 at St. James' Park on March 1, 1930, was in prospect.

Adding spice to the proceedings were the fact that City manager Bill McCracken had played for the Magpies, where he had masterminded their offside trap, and that long-throw expert Sam Weaver had moved to Newcastle from Anlaby Road only the previous November. In addition, United's Hughie Gallacher and City's Jimmy Howieson had been teammates together with Scotland and Airdrieonians. City had Matt Bell back in their side, but "Paddy" Mills was injured.

Bell, in fact, slipped as Jimmy Boyd crossed for Tommy Lang to head Newcastle in front in the 27th minute, but City stuck to their task and Gallacher, in particular, became frustrated when he was denied the space in which to manoeuvre. Another of City's Scottish internationals, Douglas "Dally" Duncan, missed two first-half chances, but he and Howieson both contributed to an equaliser for the persistent Stan Alexander, who scored with a glorious header to bring Newcastle back to Anlaby Road after 1-1 draw.

Five days later the replay attracted a record crowd of 32,930 to the ground with the winners knowing that they would face Arsenal at Elland Road, Leeds, in the semi-finals. City kept the same side, but Newcastle made four changes, including the return of their England international centre-half and £9,000 signing Jack Hill, who was later to become manager at Anlaby Road, after a two-month absence because of a difference of opinion with the club. The Newcastle party prepared for the game at Scarborough before travelling to Hull, where they stayed briefly at the Royal Station Hotel, by train on the day of the match. City, watched by the club's first manager, Ambrose Langley, reverted to their amber-and-black colours, while Newcastle, supported by about 4,000 fans, wore white shirts. Arsenal's manager Herbert Chapman and three of his players were also in the crowd.

The tie was evenly-balanced in the first half, but two minutes after the resumption City scored the only goal of the game to reach the FA Cup semi-finals for the first time. They cleared a free-kick and George Goldsmith and Ronnie Starling began a counter-attack, which ended with Billy Taylor crossing for Jimmy Howieson to score with a powerful left-foot shot from 25 yards out. It was said to be reminiscent of the goal that Howieson had scored for St. Mirren to win them the Scottish FA Cup against Celtic four years earlier and it sent the crowd wild, but there was a lot left to do. Newcastle began to attack more and more, but City found another hero, goalkeeper Fred Gibson, who denied them with a series of brilliant saves, particularly when the pressure mounted towards the end. The Tigers held on to produce one of the most memorable giantkilling acts in their history and Newcastle's player-manager Andrew Cunningham, a former Scottish international himself, said: "We lost. You have a very fine goalkeeper."

City's chairman Dr Durham Pullan was ecstatic and claimed: "With everyone in good trim for the semi-final, I don't see why we should not go to Wembley. I feel almost certain that this is to be our year." But the Tigers failed bravely in the semi-finals when they drew 2-2 with Arsenal at Elland Road and then controversially lost 1-0 to them in the replay Villa Park, home of Aston Villa. City were also relegated for the first time in their history that season and it seemed to put them off giantkilling for a while because it did not happen again until the 1948-49 season. But they made up for lost time because they produced three giantkilling episodes in a season for the only time ever. Having beaten Accrington Stanley 3-1 at home and then Reading 2-1 away after a goalless draw and extra time at Boothferry Park in the first meeting, they accounted for higher-grade opponents in three successive rounds. Second Division sides Blackburn Rovers and Grimsby Town were their first victims and then First Division Stoke City followed.

The Tigers went to Blackburn on January 8, 1949, where there were about 3,000 fans from the Hull area in a crowd of 33,200. City, who stayed overnight in Manchester – at the same hotel as the Bournemouth party who were visiting Manchester United – before the tie, were still without Raich Carter and left-winger Eddie Burbanks even though he had resumed training after an illness. Rovers made one change, bringing back left-half Eric Bell, who had missed three games because of influenza.

At that time Blackburn had won the FA Cup more than anyone else, but City, inspired by goalkeeper Billy Bly and wing-half Jimmy Greenhalgh, were to reach the fourth round for the first time for 15 years. Willie Buchan gave them the lead and it was not until ten minutes from time that Blackburn equalised through Leslie Graham to take the tie into extra time. The Tigers did not want a replay because there was a general feeling that fixture congestion might hinder their promotion push from the Third Division North and in the 91st minute Norman Moore drove in the winner from a pass by Alec Bloxham for a 2-1 success. Rovers might have created the better chances overall, but some fans had claimed that the Tigers should have had a third goal when Viggo Jensen hit the bar from 30 yards and the ball appeared to drop over the line.

The fourth round brought a derby clash at Grimsby on January 29, 1949, with City player-manager Raich Carter leaving it late to decide as to whether he had recovered sufficiently from a groin injury to play. He was needed because the Tigers were already without two other forwards, Bill Price and Eddie Burbanks. Town, who were still without injured centre-half Tom Galley, underwent indoor training at an amusement centre in Cleethorpes, where City made their overnight base before the tie. About 5,000 City fans travelled to the game on the Humber ferries – the Tattershall Castle, the Wingfield Castle and the Lincoln Castle – which started out in fog, but the sun slowly broke through. Almost 600 more fans went by train via Stainforth, while the ground staff at Blundell Park put either tar or barbed wire on fences adjoining the ground to deter people from trying to get in without paying. As it was, the attendance was 26,505.

Carter pronounced himself fit half-an-hour before the start after consulting two doctors and he was to play his part, scoring from a free-kick after Eric Sibley had handled. But the honours fell to Norman Moore, who was playing against his old club and was on the mark twice, scoring the winner after Ken Moody had miskicked. City, in fact, took the lead three times, but the Mariners, who were hampered by an injury to Billy Cairns, gallantly stayed in contention with goals by Ernie Forrest and Tommy Briggs. And there was a fright for the Tigers when Jim Whitfield had the ball in their net in the final minute, but referee Maltby gave offside. City won 3-2 to reach the fifth round for the first time for 19 years and they were also the Third Division North's last survivors in the competition.

The Tigers were rewarded with an even tougher away trip to First Division Stoke City on February 12, 1949, but they could derive confidence from the fact that they had still not been beaten in a League or cup match on their travels that season. Their supporters travelled by train, road and even by 'plane from Brough to Meir, three miles south of Stoke, and they heard on the morning of the match that the Tigers had strengthened their squad by signing goalkeeper Joe Robinson from Blackpool. City named the same side who had won at Grimsby and trainer George Lax said: "The match is going to be our hardest of the season, but I am certain we shall give Stoke a good game. I think the general public are more cup-conscious than we are ourselves. We are taking it as just another match." Stoke were without injured skipper Billy Mould and his place was taken by Jock Kirton. There was a crowd of 46,738 and heavy rain an hour before the kick-off left some standing water in the goalmouths.

City began confidently and took the lead after 20 minutes after Jimmy Greenhalgh and Viggo Jensen had initiated a move which ended with Norman Moore outjumping England international Neil Franklin, who was later to move to Boothferry Park, to plant a header in the corner of the net. Stoke were reduced to ten men for a time when Frank Mountford needed treatment for a knock and Jensen also needed attention after a clash in midfield, but the Tigers dominated the game and deserved more than just a one-goal advantage by halftime. In the end they had to settle for a 2-0 triumph after Greenhalgh had scored an amazing late goal.

The Tigers had to battle on gamely towards the end because Greenhalgh and Jensen had picked up ankle injuries and Moore had damaged a thigh, but player-manager Raich Carter said: "I am proud of the lads. Stoke officials were loud in their praise of the way we played." And years later Tom Berry told me: "I can remember that it was a very, very good game and it wasn't a fluke result. We deserved to win and, in fact, I think it was our best win of the season. We didn't think we had a cat in hell's chance, but we won and the feeling was marvellous. We could hear all the rattles and cheering as the crowd left the ground and when we stopped at a hotel

near the station, everyone was queuing up to see us. Norman Moore was one of the best headers of a ball I've known and I can still remember Jimmy Greenhalgh's goal because he bundled the ball into the net and then fell over. He was a good player and one of the funniest blokes I ever met."

Before the tie Carter had intimated that he believed that the winners would go all the way to Wembley, but he was to be proved wrong. City then faced FA Cup holders Manchester United in front of the record attendance of 55,019 at Boothferry Park, but lost 1-0 amid further controversy and their chance of reaching the semi-finals for the second time in their history evaporated. The Tigers then produced a different kind of giantkilling treble in the FA Cup because they knocked out higher-grade sides in three successive seasons for the first time.

In 1950-51 they were drawn at home to struggling Everton, who were to finish at the bottom of the First Division, in the third round. But the Toffeemen, whose manager Cliff Britton was later to have a memorable spell in charge at Boothferry Park, had staged a revival by the time that they visited City on January 6, 1951, with a return of nine points from the last 10. They were unchanged and included 41-year-old goalkeeper Ted Sagar and Harry Potts, both of whom had played in FA Cup Finals, while George Rankin and Tommy Jones were making their debuts in the competition. City, whose goalkeeper Joe Robinson had also played in an FA Cup Final with Blackpool, were without Billy Bly, who had broken his arm, but they brought back Viggo Jensen, who had recovered from a leg injury and returned at left-back in place of John Varney. Centre-half Tom Berry was passed fit after a thigh problem, while Alf Ackerman was recalled at centre-forward and Fred Smith dropped out.

Hull City's all-time great Raich Carter looks through his scrapbooks, including the club's FA Cup giantkilling heroics in 1949.

Hull City's popular defender Tom Berry.

The Tigers had been without a win since late November, but they adapted well to the sticky conditions on a pitch that had been ice-bound only a few days earlier and gave the crowd of 36,465 plenty to cheer. Everton were to be beaten 2-0 and it would have been more of an embarrassment for them if Sagar had not been on top form in goal. Raich Carter, as so often was the case that season, scored the Tigers' opening goal, but he was outshone by Eddie Burbanks, whose cross set up the second for Syd Gerrie with a header.

The Tigers then disposed of Rotherham United, who were on their way to becoming Third Division North champions, in the fourth round when they beat them 2-0 at Boothferry Park with goals by Raich Carter and Ken Harrison. But then came a piece of classic City anti-climax when they received a dose of their own medicine and were beaten 3-0 by Third Division South outfit Bristol Rovers at the fifth-round stage.

City then produced one of the greatest moments in their FA Cup giantkilling dossier in the 1951-52 season because they defeated Manchester United, who were on their way to winning the First Division title by a four-point margin from North London duo Tottenham Hotspur and Arsenal, in the third round. They were drawn away at Old Trafford on January 12, 1952, and there was a major shock in store for the 43,517 crowd. That figure might appear to be a little low by United's standards, but Manchester City were playing Wolverhampton Wanderers only a few miles away at the same time. Both sides prepared for the Old Trafford meeting by playing golf – City at Bridlington and United at Davyhulme. City, 500-to-1 outsiders to win the trophy, agreed to transfer right-winger Alan Moore to Nottingham Forest during the build-up to the tie, but Ken Harrison was available to return after recovering from a rib injury. But goalkeeper Billy Bly failed a fitness test on a damaged shoulder, so Joe Robinson made his first appearance of the season. United, for whom Roger Byrne and Ernie Bond made their cup debuts, were unchanged.

Harrison missed a great chance for City early on, but he atoned by setting up their opening goal after 15 minutes. Raich Carter began the move by beating two defenders and Harrison crossed to Syd Gerrie, who chested the ball down and scored with a firm drive. United looked as if they were going to equalise when referee Reg Leafe awarded them a penalty after Denis Durham was ruled to have fouled Bond, who had to go off for attention, as he produced a last-ditch tackle, but Jack Rowley stabbed his spot-kick wide of the post. The frenetic pace of the game did not ease up and Harrison had another good chance for City, but he chose to pass instead of shoot and it was lost. But again he redeemed himself when he made it 2-0 in the 42nd minute, shooting into the roof of the net from a tight angle after the lively Eddie Burbanks had centred from the touchline. That was how it stayed although City had to defend desperately in the second half, but Robinson, Durham and Tom Berry were outstanding. And on the final whistle United's manager Matt Busby immediately made his way from his seat in the stand to tell the Tigers: "Well done. You deserved it."

Their cup run made no further headway, though, because City lost 2-0 at Blackburn Rovers, who were to finish just four places above them in the Second Division that season, in the fourth round. But City's trilogy of giantkilling feats in consecutive seasons was completed in the third round of the 1952-53 FA Cup when they were drawn at home to Charlton Athletic, who were emerging as a leading force in the First Division that season.

The tie attracted a crowd of 37,531 to Boothferry Park on January 10, 1953, and City manager Bob Jackson was confident of victory after he, Neil Franklin, Viggo Jensen and Tom Berry had seen Charlton in action, but he sought the help of the fans and asked: "What about the Boothferry Roar being revived? Our boys are only human and will respond to any spur that the crowd can give them." The Tigers were without Franklin and Ted Tarrant, while Berry pulled out with a leg injury and Wilf Hassall took his place. Jackson opted to give a home debut to left-winger Brian Cripsey even though Eddie Burbanks had recovered from a pulled muscle. Charlton's manager Jimmy Seed was plagued by injury worries, but in the end John Hewie, Derek Ufton, Gordon Hurst and Charlie Vaughan were all passed fit although Bobby Ayre, Billy Kiernan and Chris Duffy were ruled out, so left-winger Kevin Barry was given his debut.

The Tigers got off to a great start when they took the lead after just 12 minutes. Jensen and Ufton jostled for the ball and when it ran clear, Bill Harris stepped in to score from 20 yards with a shot that gave Charlton goalkeeper Sam Bartram no chance. The breakthrough came immediately after Eddie Firmani had hit the woodwork for Athletic at the other end and soon afterwards they had another setback when Vaughan suffered injuries to both ankles. With Andy Davidson and Ernie Phillips solid in defence, City were in command and they made it 2-0 in the 42nd minute when Jensen scored from the penalty spot after a handling offence. Ken Horton added a third early in the second half and it was not until the closing stages that Stuart Leary grabbed a consolation goal for Charlton. It ended 3-1 and Seed intriguingly told the City camp afterwards: "You have tasted the sweet wines of success the day and I wish you all the good luck I had hoped for myself."

Viggo Jensen, the Great Dane who was Hull City's penalty hero in the FA Cup against Charlton Athletic in January 1953.

But, as was the case two seasons earlier, City's FA Cup hopes ended in humiliation because they were knocked out by Gateshead, then in the Third Division North, at the fourth-round stage. The Tigers lost 2-1 at home as they again went unceremoniously from the FA Cup sublime to the ridiculous in the same season.

And it was not until the Tigers themselves had descended into the Third Division North that they produced another FA Cup shock. It came in the 1957-58 season after their cup run had started with a 2-1 home win over Crewe Alexandra with goals by Bill Bradbury and Doug Clarke and then two second-round meetings with Port Vale. Bradbury and Andy Davidson scored in a 2-2 draw at Vale Park and then City won 4-3 in a dramatic replay, which included a stoppage because of a power cut, after extra time. Bradbury was twice on the mark this time, his close friend Brian Bulless also scored and Bill Cleary put through his own goal. That earned the Tigers a third-round tie at home to Second Division Barnsley on January 4, 1958, and they were to get through the hard way.

The clash at Boothferry Park was doubtful for a time because of the combined effect of rain, snow and frost on the pitch, but a crowd of 21,868 turned out. City retained Bernard Fisher in goal, right-winger Johnny Stephens passed a fitness check on an ankle that he had injured in training and Brian Cripsey returned on the left-wing after more than a month on the sidelines with a damaged calf. Barnsley were at full strength.

City almost led after just 45 seconds when Bradbury landed a header on the bar, but he was not to be subdued and did score in the third minute. Denis Durham and Bulless combined to send Bradbury racing through the middle and he hammered his shot over the advancing Harry Hough. The Tigers were the better side, but Barnsley equalised after 20 minutes following a foul on Arthur Kaye. Les Collinson initially cleared John Short's free-kick, but Larratt Chappell slipped the ball to Norman Smith, who volleyed home. City continued to pile on the pressure and created the better opportunities, but it finished 1-1 and that meant a replay at Oakwell four days later.

The Tigers, who regarded Oakwell as one of their unlucky grounds, were unchanged for the replay after Fisher had recovered from a damaged shoulder and Davidson had passed a fitness test on a bruised shin. But Barnsley's manager Tim Ward made one change, bringing in promising teenager Frank Beaumont in place of transfer-listed inside-forward Malcolm Graham.

The crowd of 20,890 were to witness an upset as City again took the game by the scruff of the neck and adapted quickly to the pitch that had become very soft after heavy rain. They again scored an early goal and all five forwards played a part in the build-up after just three minutes. Cripsey and Bulless began the move on the left, Bradbury switched play to the right, Johnny Stephens clipped the ball inside and Doug Clarke hooked his shot home. Barnsley temporarily lost winger Arthur Kaye after a tackle by Durham and went further behind while they were reduced to ten men. In the 21st minute Bulless went on a solo run and, although his attempted cross was blocked by Short, he quickly fastened on to the loose ball to score his first goal of the season. Barnsley began to apply more and more pressure, but they could make little headway and Bulless almost added a third early in the second half when his powerful drive rattled the bar.

It stayed 2-0 to cheer City chairman Harold Needler, who had missed only his third cup tie in 35 years because of a bout of pneumonia, and they earned themselves another Yorkshire derby against Sheffield Wednesday, who were relegated when they finished at the bottom of the First Division that season. And the Owls were made to fight all the way to beat City 4-3 in front of a 51,834 crowd at Hillsborough in the fourth round. Bradbury made it six goals from six games in the FA Cup that season, while Bulless and Stephens were also on the mark for the Tigers.

The Tigers did not produce a further FA Cup shock until another of their all-too-brief golden eras when they reached the quarter-finals in the 1965-66 season amid their successful assault on the Third Division title. But it consisted of a double act in the third and fourth rounds as they knocked out Southampton, who were to be promoted as the runners-up to Manchester City in the Second Division, and Nottingham Forest, then in the First Division, respectively.

During the build-up to the clash with Southampton at Boothferry Park on January 22, 1966 – a remarkably late date for a third-round tie – City announced plans to redevelop the club's best stand, but they barely came to fruition. The Tigers kept the same side who had beaten Workington 6-0 a week earlier, while

Hull City's promotion heroes line up before their FA Cup giantkilling episode against Southampton in January 1966. They are (left to right): Dennis Butler, Ray Henderson, Alan Jarvis, Ken Wagstaff, Ian Butler, Ken Houghton, Andy Davidson, Maurice Swan, Chris Chilton, Chris Simpkin, Mick Milner.

Southampton manager Ted Bates preferred 20-year-old Norman Dean in a forward-line also including Terry Paine, Jimmy Melia and Martin Chivers. George O'Brien was still ill, so Dean got the nod ahead of David Walker.

The crowd of 28,851 saw a tie that was played in difficult conditions because of swirling fog and a tricky, heavily-sanded surface following a sudden thaw. The game went ahead only after some inspections by referee Ken Dagnall, but City adjusted well and Southampton had some lucky escapes when Ian Butler, Ken Houghton and Ken Wagstaff all hit the woodwork. It took them a long time to break the stalemate, though, and it was not until the 77th minute that Houghton scored the only goal of the game with a cool finish after Wagstaff and Chris Chilton had engineered the opening. The Saints then mounted a determined onslaught for an equaliser and the Tigers had to hang on grimly in the closing stages.

Houghton reflected: "There was a thin coating of snow still on the pitch and the conditions were far from easy. I'd probably like to think that my terrific speed took me past six defenders in the build-up to the goal, but in reality it came from a through ball by 'Waggy' to me in the inside-right position. The Southampton 'keeper Campbell Forsyth made my mind up for me and I seem to recall that I just slipped my shot inside the post."

The fourth-round tie against Nottingham Forest on February 12, 1966, was also at Boothferry Park and attracted an impressive crowd of 38,055. In fact, the police had asked fans to leave their cars at home and use public transport to ease parking and congestion. Both sides were below strength for the tie and City's plans were hit by repeated doubts about their line-up. It began with worries about goalkeeper Maurice Swan, who was ill, and Ken Wagstaff, who had suffered a bruised foot in a 1-0 home win over Brighton and Hove Albion in the League. As the week progressed, left-back Dennis Butler damaged a foot in a training accident in the club's gymnasium and he was ruled out. His place went to Mike Brown, more

recently Manchester United's chief scout, but even though Swan and Wagstaff recovered, there was to be another last-minute hitch. Shortly before the game Chris Simpkin, who was otherwise an ever-present that season, dropped out after pulling a muscle in training, so Terry Heath was drafted into his place. Forest's manager Johnny Carey had to bring in centre-half Bill Taylor because Bob McKinlay was forced to miss his first cup tie for the club for 15 years. He was also without Colin Addison and Frank Wignall, so Bob Chapman and teenager Barry McArthur continued as their deputies.

Terry Heath was playing his first game for City for five months, but he made

Hull City's Chris Chilton puts in an aerial challenge on Southampton goalkeeper Campbell Forsyth during their FA Cup meeting In January 1966. The Saints' centre-half Tony Knapp provides extra cover.

Terry Heath beats Nottingham Forest goalkeeper Peter Grummitt and defender Peter Hindley to score the opening goal in Hull City's shock 2-0 win in the FA Cup at Boothferry Park in February 1966.

the most of it to stamp his name indelibly in the annals of the club's cup tie history. His inclusion, in fact, had almost been the last resort for manager Cliff Britton when Simpkin pulled out on the morning of the match. He initially wanted to bring in Les Collinson, but found that he had gone to bed with influenza: he then tried to contact Len Sharpe with telephone and telegram messages, but he was somewhere between his home in Scunthorpe and the ground. Britton finally turned to Heath, who, quite simply, scored both goals as the Tigers sensationally won 2-0. His first came after 20 minutes when he showed great tenacity to seize on to a weak back-pass by Peter Hindley to slip the ball past goalkeeper Peter Grummitt. City had the chances to increase their lead, but it was not until nine minutes from the end that they sealed victory when Wagstaff's centre found Chris Chilton and he teed the ball up for Heath to score with a shot from the edge of the penalty area.

Curiously, Heath, though, has always had reservations about the game and its aftermath because he said:"I can't remember much about the game. For the first goal I got on to a backpass and the second was a shot from the edge of the box, but I didn't think that I had a particularly good game. I scored the goals and that was it. I appreciated every goal I scored in my career, but at the same time I would always rather have a good game than score goals. And on this occasion I was dropped the next week against Queen's Park Rangers. That was the most disappointing part of it because it was a bitter pill at the end of it all."

And while Heath stole the limelight, it was generally agreed that Ken Houghton, who slotted into a more defensive role in Simpkin's absence, was the best player on the park. Houghton was an equally reluctant hero, though, because he insisted: "It was one of the easiest games in which I ever played. I played what was to become

known as the sweeper's role – I was able to read the game, I was given plenty of room and I was allowed time to use the ball well. I wouldn't say that it was my best game for the club and I do get a bit annoyed at times when people come up to me and say that's how they remember it. I hardly made a mistake against Forest, but then I always felt that I did well against First Division opposition. We did a great job tactically against Forest and that was because Cliff Britton's knowledge showed through. I admired Cliff so much as a manager, but I can remember that after the match he slated us and knocked me off my pedestal. I'd hit one bad pass and Cliff brought me down to earth when we met to discuss the match the following Tuesday because he kept harping on about it. I've never known such a perfectionist."

City then had to work hard to beat Fourth Division Southport, their fellow giantkillers that season, 2-0 in the fifth round, but two-goal Chris Chilton saw them through after a rare penalty miss by Ken Houghton. Then another FA Cup run ended in hotly-disputed fashion when they drew 2-2 at Chelsea and then lost 3-1 at Boothferry Park in the replay at the quarter-final stage.

The Tigers next produced an FA Cup action replay 20 years ago. In successive seasons in 1950-51, 1951-52 and 1952-53 they had produced one giant-killing act: curiously, they did so again in 1970-71, 1971-72 and 1972-73 to land another notable treble.

In 1970-71 they again reached the quarter-finals before going out controversially when Stoke City beat them 3-2 at Boothferry Park. In the third round City

Terry Heath (far left) threads home his shot for the second goal in Hull City's 2-0 win over Nottingham Forest in the FA Cup at Boothferry Park in February 1966. His teammates Ray Henderson (left) and Chris Chilton look on.

Chris Chilton (third from left) competes with his own team-mate Malcolm Lord and the Blackpool defence to head in one of Hull City's goals in their 2-0 home win in the FA Cup in January 1971. The Tigers' Ken Wagstaff (left) and Terry Neill watch the action.

had played some magical soccer in snowy conditions to beat Charlton Athletic 3-0 at Boothferry Park with goals by Ken Wagstaff, Ken Houghton and Ian Butler. Two rounds later they had to come from behind to avoid being on the receiving end of a cup upset of their own when they defeated mid-table Fourth Division side Brentford 2-1 with goals by Houghton and Chris Chilton. But in-between they accounted for Blackpool, who were to end up being relegated from the First Division that season when they propped it up, in front of a 34,752 gate at Boothferry Park in the fourth round on January 23, 1971.

The Tigers prepared for the game at Scarborough, where they stood on the terraces to watch the locals beat Witton Albion 3-0 in the FA Trophy, while Blackpool left their own seaside to get ready for the tie at Filey! City player-manager Terry Neill relegated Houghton to substitute after Wagstaff had been passed fit to return after a knee injury, while Blackpool's manager Bob Stokoe gave a debut to former Oxford Blue Peter Suddaby in place of Micky Burns with Tony Coleman switching to the left-wing.

Blackpool, who included former England full-back Jimmy Armfield, had remained unbeaten under Stokoe's management since his move to Bloomfield Road from Carlisle United, but they got a shock in an uncompromising battle in which Chris Simpkin stood out for the Tigers. While the Seasiders were briefly down to ten men when Dave Hatton left the field for treatment to a facial wound, City took the lead, Chris Chilton flicking home an inswinging corner by Ian Butler ten

minutes before halftime. Ten minutes after halftime it was 2-0 when Ken Wagstaff headed home a cross from Simpkin and that was how it stayed although City full-back Frank Banks later had to go off because of a head wound of his own.

Stokoe's sides had generally done well against City, so that ghost was easily exorcised. But chairman Harold Needler put the giantkilling act uncompromisingly into context because the Tigers were also doing well in the League in Terry Neill's first season in charge and he insisted: "This was the least important game on our fixture list. Our main ambition must be to gain promotion to the First Division."

Norwich City, though, were able to be single-minded on their way to the Second Division title in 1971-72 when they went out of the FA Cup in the third round, emphatically losing 3-0 at Carrow Road to the Tigers, whose goals were scored by Ken Wagstaff, Ian Butler and Jimmy McGill. That brought them a trip to First Division Coventry City in the fourth round on February 5, 1972, and a reunion with one of their all-time greats, Chris Chilton. City player-manager Terry Neill had sold Chilton to Coventry for £92,000 soon after the start of the season: now he found himself having to mark him in a cup tie!

City, whose pre-match build-up included a trip to ATV's studios in Birmingham

Ken Wagstaff heads home one of Hull City's goals in their shock 2-0 win over Blackpool in the FA Cup at Boothferry Park in January 1971.

to watch a film of Coventry in action, brought in experienced defender Bill Baxter for his first full game of the season and switched Billy Wilkinson into midfield as the replacement for suspended skipper Ken Knighton. Coventry brought in Mick Coop at right-back to enable Wilf Smith to move into midfield alongside Ian St. John in place of the injured Ernie Machin, while top scorer Ernie Hunt returned in attack. The crowd of 24,621 included England's manager Sir Alf Ramsey.

The Highfield Road pitch was very heavy because it had just recovered from having four inches of snow on it and the tie rarely reached the high level that might have been expected of it with chances few and far between. Hunt had one effort disallowed when he had the ball in the net only to discover that referee Ron Challis had pulled play back for a free-kick to Coventry, but City were otherwise largely untroubled and 13 minutes from time they grabbed the only goal of the game. Malcolm Lord gained possession when Coventry's goalkeeper Bill Glazier punched out a cross from Ian Butler and set up Frank Banks, whose shot struck the inside of the post. But that ace goal-poacher Ken Wagstaff got to the rebound first to grab his fourth goal in four matches and the Tigers were through.

Wagstaff was given a sky-blue carnation by City chairman Harold Needler's wife Hilary – it had been presented to her before the tie by Coventry supremo Derrick Robins – for scoring the winner and Chilton was magnanimous in defeat against his old sparring partners because he said:"I never underestimated my old side. The defence played very well and although we had more of the play, I would think that City had the better chances and more of them. It was anyone's game until 'Waggy' scored and I feel a bit sick about it because there's nothing left for us to play for now."

In the fifth round the Tigers, forced to play defender John Kaye in his original position as a centre-forward because of injuries, were beaten 4-1 by First Division Stoke City at the Victoria Ground. The Potters, therefore, knocked City, for whom Wagstaff scored for the third FA Cup tie in a row, out of the competition for the second successive season.

But in 1972-73 the Tigers were back with another FA Cup shock when they met West Ham United, then a prominent First Division force, in the fourth round. City had made hard work of it to get that far because they drew 0-0 in a bruising battle at Fourth Division Stockport County in the third round before beating them 2-0 with extra-time goals by Ken Wagstaff and Ken Houghton in the replay. Houghton, though, was to play an even more significant role in the meeting with the Hammers.

City, who prepared for the tie at Scarborough, were without Wagstaff for the West Ham tie because of a knee injury, so Phil Holme continued to deputise, while midfield man Ken Knighton came through a fitness test on a groin problem. West Ham's manager Ron Greenwood, who knew his City counterpart Terry Neill from their time together at Arsenal, named an unchanged side, who included Bobby Moore, Trevor Brooking and Bryan "Pop" Robson, then the First Division's leading goalscorer.

The Tigers took the game to the Hammers and harried them constantly, winning nine corners in the first half. And they got a breakthrough in the 29th minute when Houghton pounced for an opportunist goal after United's goalkeeper Bobby Ferguson and Bobby Moore had been caught out. "I can't remember much

about the goal except that Stuart Pearson and Phil Holme were involved and put West Ham under pressure. The ball ran free and all I had to do was to side-foot it home," he said. The tie died a little as the second half wore on, but referee Norman Burtenshaw seemed to play an inordinate amount of injury time to keep most of the 32,290 fans on tenterhooks and City had to endure one almighty goalmouth melee before goalkeeper Ian McKechnie emerged clutching the ball.

Times had changed for City chairman Harold Needler because he recalled crying 50 years earlier after West Ham had beaten his boyhood heroes 3-2 in the FA Cup at Anlaby Road and had insisted that there would be no chance of a repeat reaction on this occasion! Houghton, meanwhile, had exacted his own personal revenge because he had suffered a painful injury when the Tigers had lost 1-0 to the Hammers in the Football League Cup in 1970: "I pulled a muscle as I ran between Bobby Moore and Frank Lampard to try to reach a through ball and I suddenly shot into the air with the pain. Terry Neill sent me to Highbury straightaway to get treatment from the Arsenal physiotherapist Fred Street and they had me jogging again the next morning, so I've got far better memories of the FA Cup tie when we beat them."

But in the fifth round the Tigers were well-beaten 3-0 by First Division Coventry City, who gained quick and ample revenge for their embarrassing exit at Highfield Road the previous season. And it is indicative of City's general decline towards the end of the 20th century that they were to go on the longest run in their history without pulling off an FA Cup giantkilling act. It was not until December 5, 1998, that

Ken Houghton (far right) waits to pounce for the only goal of Hull City's FA Cup giantkilling victory over West Ham United at Boothferry Park in February 1973. The Hammers' goalkeeper Booby Ferguson can only push the ball away under pressure from City's Stuart Pearson.

Ken Houghton turns to celebrate his goal. His teammates Ken Knighton (far left) and Roy Greenwood (far right) also hail the winner.

the Tigers were to give their fans something to special to cheer again in the competition as they defied the odds.

City were facing an uphill battle to maintain their League status after slumping to the bottom of the current Third Division, but they gained some respite from it in the FA Cup. In the first round they overcame Dr Marten's League side Salisbury City with a 2-0 victory thanks to goals by Gregor Rioch and Brian McGinty and were then drawn away to Second Division Luton Town, who had already beaten Barnsley, Coventry City and Ipswich Town at Kenilworth Road on their way to the Worthington Cup quarter-finals that season. And a shock seemed even more unlikely because of City's poor League form and the fact that Warren Joyce had only recently taken over as player-manager in succession to Mark Hateley.

In addition, the Tigers were without nine first-team regulars and they were forced to make five changes from the side who had beaten Carlisle United 1-0 in the League a week earlier. Paul Gibson, Craig Dudley, Steve Hawes, Gareth Williams and Joyce himself were all missing and Steve Wilson, Mark Greaves, Jon French, Ben Morley and Brian McGinty were called up. Joyce, sidelined with back trouble, also had to put five youngsters on the substitutes' bench, so the omens generally were not good. Luton, meanwhile, brought in Matthew Spring for Mitchell Thomas, while leading marksman Phil Gray passed a fitness check on an ankle problem.

The crowd of 5,021 were in for a shock on a bitterly cold afternoon, though. Teenager Ben Morley had to play up front because of the selection difficulties and the move paid off in the 29th minute when he put City ahead. David d'Auria and David Brown made the running down the right and, when the ball came over, Morley lashed home a low, first-time shot. Six minutes later, though, Luton's captain Steve Davis equalised right on cue after exchanging passes with Gary Doherty. City defender Justin Whittle hit the post at the other end, but it was still 1-1 at halftime and both sides created good chances soon after the resumption. The Tigers, however, regained the lead after 64 minutes following a foul by Alan White on Morley. d'Auria sent over the free-kick from the right and the Hatters' defence left City defender Rob Dewhurst unmarked to head home at the far post.

City hung on for a 2-1 triumph and were then drawn against Aston Villa at Villa Park in the third round. At the time of the game Villa were top of the FA Premiership and the Tigers were rooted at the bottom of the Third Division. They could not bridge the gap, but put on a respectable show in going down 3-0 in front of 39,217 fans.

It is also worth recording, of course, that another avenue of cup interest opened up in 1960 – the Football League Cup – and City went out of it to Bolton Wanderers in the year of its inception. But in 1961-62 it provided the Tigers with another giantkilling act.

They beat Bradford Park Avenue 4-2 at home in the first round when Chris Chilton (two) and Charlie Crickmore scored and ex-Tiger Charlie Atkinson put through his own goal. They were then drawn away to Second Division Bury at Gigg Lane on October 3, 1961. The Tigers, who had lost only once in 11 outings, were unchanged for the seventh time in a row, while the Shakers had Michael Brennan and Brian Eastham in defence in place of the injured Brian Gallagher and Les Riggs, while right-winger Billy Calder replaced Allan Jackson.

The game was to be a thriller and remains the only occasion on which City have scored four goals on their travels in the Football League Cup. And they had to produce an amazing fightback to seal their victory because they were 2-0 and 3-1 down at different stages. Bury took the lead on the half-hour when Bill Holden flicked home a cross from the powerful Gordon Atherton and Frank Beaumont added a second two minutes before the break following a goalmouth scramble, but Les Collinson cracked home a 25-yard drive 30 seconds later to keep the Tigers in contention at the interval. Bernard Fisher had already performed heroics in goal for a below-par City, but he had no chance in the 55th minute when Andy Davidson deflected another fierce shot by Beaumont past him to leave Bury 3-1 ahead. But then the Tigers stirred and the Shakers were well and truly shaken. After 59 minutes Chilton made it 3-2 when he picked up a loose clearance by Bobby Conroy to score. Bury applied some more pressure, but City refused to wilt under it and they completed a stunning 4-3 success with further goals in the 80th and 82nd minutes. Doug Clarke, who had joined City from Bury, hooked home an awkwardly-bouncing ball from Crickmore's pass to equalise and then Chilton headed the winner from a centre by Brian Bulless to the chagrin of most of the 8,204 crowd.

The Tigers went out of the competition at the third-round stage even though John McSeveney scored against his old club in a 2-1 defeat at Second Division promotion challengers Sunderland. But City had shown their capabilities in the competition and the following season they were to defy the odds to beat one of the North-East's big sides in it. In 1962-63 they did not enter the competition until the second round and they were drawn at home to Middlesbrough, then one of the Second Division's leading sides, on September 24, 1962. City were unchanged for the fifth successive game with Ray Henderson facing his old club, while Middlesbrough's centre-forward Alan Peacock had been in England's World Cup squad that year.

City almost pulled off a shock at the first time of asking in front of a 10,640 attendance because they produced a fine performance and only an 88th-minute equaliser spared Middlesbrough's blushes. The Tigers took an 11th-minute lead when Chris Chilton capitalised on a weak backpass by Dick Neal and his shot went in off the post and they went further ahead in the 39th minute when Les Collinson volleyed home Eric McMillan's cross. City might have had everything sewn up if had not been for 'Boro' goalkeeper Arthur Lightening's brilliance, while Henderson twice hit the post. And the Tigers still looked comfortable when Ron Burbeck pulled back a goal with a far-post header from Arthur Kaye's cross in the 63rd minute. But Middlesbrough hung on to mount one last rally and Burbeck rescued them when he made it 2-2 with his second goal.

It was not until October 8, 1962, that the replay took place in front of 15,612 fans. There was bound to be some consternation as to whether City, who again fielded an unchanged side, had let their best chance of going through slip through their grasp, while they had lost 5-1 and 4-0 against Middlesbrough on their most recent trips to face them at Ayresome Park. 'Boro' included four players who had not been involved in the first meeting – Neville Chapman, Bill Gates, Joe Livingstone, who took over from the injured Peacock, and recent signing Bobby Hume.

Middlesbrough dominated much of the first half, but it was not until a minute before halftime that they broke the deadlock when Ray Yeoman and Bryan Orritt carved out the chance for Ian Gibson to score. City played much better in the second half, but they had to wait until the 82nd minute before they grabbed an equaliser. Doug Clarke had scored twice in a 2-2 draw at Colchester in the League two days earlier and he came up trumps again when he drove the ball home from John McSeveney's corner. The tie went into extra time when the Tigers looked the more likely to grab a winner, but it ended 1-1.

A coin was tossed to decide who were to have home advantage in the second replay and City chairman Harold Needler won it in competition with Middlesbrough's manager Bob Dennison, so the action reverted to Boothferry Park two days later when there was a gate of 11,964. The Tigers were finally forced to make a change because Brian Bulless had a stomach-muscle injury, so the versatile Len Sharpe, a close-season signing from Scunthorpe United, took his place at left-back. 'Boro' brought in Derek Stonehouse at left-back in place of Gordon Jones, while they made four changes in the forward-line. Kaye, Orritt and Gibson were injured and Livingstone was omitted with Burbeck, Don Walker, ex-Tiger Bill Harris and teenager Peter Bryan being called up.

The tie was to prove eventful for Bill Harris because he had to deputise in goal for Lightening, who went off with a back problem in the 57th minute. Lightening had repeatedly denied the Tigers during the three ties and he had rescued Middlesbrough again on this occasion when they conceded a 39th-minute penalty after Bill Gates had brought down Chilton. Lightening saved Andy Davidson's spot-kick and then did well to keep out McSeveney's follow-up attempt and, although City applied a lot of pressure, it was still 0-0 after 90 minutes. Harris had performed the same emergency task in goal in his City days, but he and his colleagues finally succumbed in extra time. The breakthrough came in the 101st minute when Chilton headed a corner from Clarke goalwards and the ball appeared to be handled, but McSeveney made sure as the Tigers appealed for another penalty. City then eased their way to a clear-cut 3-0 victory with goals by Dudley Price and Chilton after 109 and 119 minutes respectively and the cup marathon was finally over.

But the Tigers must have wondered whether it was worth all the trouble because their interest in the competition ended in the third round when 20,308 fans saw them entertain First Division Fulham at Boothferry Park and they lost 2-1 despite a goal by Chilton.

It was to be a long time before City pulled off another giantkilling act in the Football League Cup. This time their second-round victims were Leicester City: they were also a First Division side and the Tigers again needed a replay to get through. Both meetings produced plenty of goals and City were unlucky not to go through at the first attempt when they went to Filbert Street on October 8, 1973, for a tie that attracted an attendance of 9,777.

City, for whom Malcolm Lord was still ruled out, switched Jimmy McGill to left-back instead of the injured Roger de Vries and brought in Chris Galvin in midfield, while Leicester were without defender Graham Cross because of a pulled muscle, but Dennis Rofe, Alan Birchenall and Mike Stringfellow all passed late fitness tests.

Peter Shilton conceded a remarkable number of goals against the Tigers during the lengthy career – he was also sent off at Boothferry Park when he was Plymouth Argyle's player-manager – and he was twice caught in the first half on this occasion. After four minutes he fumbled a centre by Frank Banks and Steve Whitworth hooked the ball into his own net as he tried to clear. And then City went 2-0 ahead on the half-hour when Shilton made a hash of dealing with a fierce drive from John Hawley and Ken Wagstaff was left with a simple chance to score. John Kaye typically battled on after crashing into a post in one defensive scramble and the Tigers survived until the 50th minute when Keith Weller pulled back a goal after Rofe and Birchenall had created the opening. But five minutes later it was 3-1 when Galvin supported an attack involving Wagstaff and Stuart Pearson and unleashed a 30-yard drive that deflected into the net off Birchenall. City might have had another goal when Banks hit the post from close range, but Leicester again reduced the arrears when Whitworth's lob was headed back by Stringfellow headed back for Frank Worthington to hook the ball home. And in injury time the Tigers had to settle for a 3-3 draw when Weller powerfully headed in a cross from Leicester's substitute John Farrington.

de Vries was to make the most of his return to City's side for the replay at Boothferry Park 23 days later, while Lord was also back in action by then. Pearson played even though he had been doubtful because of illness, but Kaye was missing after receiving a severe thigh injury – the legacy of a savage tackle on him by John Craggs in a League game at Middlesbrough. Leicester included Alan Woollett at right-back instead of Whitworth, while Cross was back in defence in place of Malcolm Manley.

It is probably fair to say that the normally-reliable Shilton was not having the best spell of his career because he had been blamed in part for the crucial goal conceded by England in a 1-1 draw with Poland at Wembley in a vital World Cup qualifier between Leicester's two ties involving the Tigers. Leicester went ahead after just two minutes of the replay in front of 16,003 fans when City goalkeeper Jeff Wealands dropped Worthington's header from Rofe's cross and Stringfellow scored. But in the 10th minute de Vries equalised when he took Roy Greenwood's pass and scored from 30 yards with Shilton strangely rooted to the spot. No-one was really sure whether it was a shot or a cross from de Vries: he was just happy to make sure that he had picked a top-drawer international goalkeeper to beat for what was his only senior goal for the Tigers! After 27 minutes Leicester regained the lead when Len Glover crossed and Stringfellow returned the compliment for Worthington to score, but on the stroke of halftime the outstanding Greenwood glanced a header in off the post from Banks' free-kick to make it 2-2. The tempo of the game decreased in the second half, but four minutes from the end City stole a winner when Pearson raced on to a long kick by Wealands and scored with a spectacular shot.

In the third round City beat Stockport County, who were destined to prop up the Fourth Division that season, 4-1 at Boothferry Park with goals by Phil Holme (two), Ken Wagstaff and Frank Banks. Then came a plum tie at home to mighty Liverpool in the fourth round. It ended in a goalless draw on a tricky surface at Boothferry Park and Liverpool won the replay 3-1, the Tigers scoring thanks to an own goal by Alec Lindsay.

Two seasons later the Tigers dumped Sheffield United out of the Football League Cup after having beaten Preston North End 4-2 at home at the second-round stage. Malcolm Lord scored a classic goal after a magnificent build-up and Roy Greenwood (two) and Alf Wood were also on the mark. That earned City a home tie against the troubled Blades in the third round.

It took place on October 7, 1975, and the pre-match tension was augmented by backroom changes at both clubs. In City's case there was a boardroom shake-up with Henry Needler and Ron Buttery stepping down to become the club's president and vice-president respectively. Hilary Needler was made patron and Trevor Thomas, Malcolm Kay, Bob Chapman and Geoffrey Needler all became directors. United, for their part, were bottom of the First Division and sacked manager Ken Furphy the day before the tie, putting former player Cec Coldwell in caretaker charge.

City manager John Kaye had problems in midfield because Malcolm Lord, Vince Grimes and Stuart Blampey were already sidelined and Chris Galvin was then ruled out because of a thigh strain. He brought back teenager Dave Stewart for only his second first-team outing and gave Ken Wagstaff his first start for almost two months after knee trouble, but left Peter Daniel out of the starting line-up. United also had their problems because Len Badger was suspended and Cliff Calvert was cup tied, while Eddie Colquhoun, Steve Faulkner, Steve Goulding and Billy Dearden were all injured. In addition, Coldwell dropped striker Tony Field, but Colin Franks, Keith Eddy, David Bradford and Chris Guthrie were all fit to return.

The Tigers had gone 346 minutes without scoring, but it did not take them long to break the deadlock because they went ahead after eight minutes when Roy Greenwood scored his third goal in two games in the competition, picking up a loose ball after Alf Wood had challenged for John Hawley's centre. And it was 2-0 to City in the 35th minute when Frank Banks crossed from the right and the ball eventually fell to Hawley, who outwitted two defenders before calmly slotting it home. That was how it stayed even though Tony Currie desperately tried to get the Blades going. But Wagstaff was outstanding in an unaccustomed midfield role and Stewart was also a revelation as City had overcome their difficulties better than United and most of the 9,536 fans went home happy.

City then had a great opportunity to progress further in the competition when they faced another Yorkshire derby in the fourth round. But they went to Doncaster Rovers, dominated the game and still lost 2-1.

In 1982-83 City again beat Sheffield United in the Football League Cup, but they did not knock them out. The two-legged first-round format meant that the Tigers went out 3-2 on aggregate. They lost 3-1 at Bramall Lane in the first leg, but a goal by Andy Flounders gave them a 1-0 victory in the second at Boothferry Park. And the same situation recurred in the 1993-94 season when City beat First Division Notts County 3-1 at home in the second leg of the first round of what was by then the Coca Cola Cup. But they had lost the first leg 2-0 at Meadow Lane and Mark Draper's away goal in the second meeting saw County through.

There was also the same kind of anomaly in the Full Members' Cup in the 1985-86 season when City, then in the Second Division, met First Division Manchester City in the Northern Area Final over two legs. The Tigers won the first leg 2-1 at

Boothferry Park on November 26, 1985, with goals by Frank Bunn and Stan McEwan. Manchester City's marksman was David Phillips, whose teammate Jim Melrose, it was reported, was carried off with a knee injury, dropped off the stretcher as he was taken behind the West Stand and immediately treated for concussion as a priority instead! It did not do him much lasting harm, however, because he and Phillips were on the mark in the second leg at Maine Road on December 11 when the Tigers lost 2-0 to go out 3-2 on aggregate. But it stands as a big anti-climax in City's history because it has been the closest that they had ever come to a trip to Wembley: as it was, Manchester City beat Chelsea 5-4 in the final.

In 1991-92, however, the Tigers caused another surprise when they knocked out Blackburn Rovers, who were beginning to build on the back of benefactor Jack Walker's investments, in the first round of what was then known as the Rumbelow's Cup. City, who were without midfield player Mick Matthews after he had fractured a bone in his leg in his first League game for the club, gave themselves a chance of causing a surprise when they drew 1-1 in the first leg at Ewood Park. They had to come from behind because defender Neil Buckley put through his own goal in the 24th minute when he sliced a cross from Rovers' midfield man Steve Agnew past goalkeeper Alan Fettis. But the Tigers were level after 57 minutes when Andy Payton took a pass from Mark Calvert and coolly rounded Rovers' goalkeeper Bobby Mimms to score with a shot that went in off a post. It set things up nicely for the second leg.

The Tigers, who who left out Mark Calvert, David Mail and Neil Buckley and recalled defender Gary Hobson, had a vital away goal to their name as they went into the second leg at Boothferry Park, but they did not need it because Blackburn could not score one themselves. And the Tigers got through 2-1 on aggregate with a 1-0 victory when they scored on the hour. Hobson broke up a move by Rovers and linked with Leigh Palin, whose accurate long ball found left-winger Leigh Jenkinson, who placed his drive confidently in the far corner of the net.

City went out 8-1 on aggregate to Queen's Park Rangers in the second round, losing 3-0 at home and going down 5-1 at Loftus Road in the second meeting. But they had embar-

Leigh Jenkinson, whose goal enabled Hull City to knock Blackburn Rovers out of the Rumbelow's Cup in August 1991.

rassed Blackburn because soon afterwards they changed managers, sacking Don Mackay and installing Kenny Dalglish in his place.

The Tigers' giantkilling exploits were slowly becoming more and more rare, but then in successive seasons they caused upsets in the Coca Cola Cup. On both occasions City were a struggling side in the Third Division, but they accounted for FA

Premiership side Crystal Palace in the second round in 1997-98 and then First Division Stockport County in the first round in 1998-99 to bring some badly-needed joy to their long-suffering fans.

City earned a two-legged battle with Palace after defeating League newcomers Macclesfield Town in the first round. They drew 0-0 on their first visit to Macclesfield and then won the second leg 2-1 after extra time with goals by Richard Peacock and Warren Joyce. Palace were respectably placed in the Premiership when they met the Tigers even though they were to be relegated at the end of the season.

The first leg was at Boothferry Park on September 16, 1997, and City chairman Tim Wilby stepped down after only a brief tenure of office as a prelude to the game with the club's owner David Lloyd replacing him. City's player-manager Mark Hateley included himself in the side even though he admitted that he was not 100 per cent fit because of a groin injury, while Neil Mann returned after groin trouble and Antonio Doncel was back after suspension, but Glyn Hodges was ruled out because of a calf problem. Palace were without the injured Attilio Lombardo, their Italian star, and Paul Warhurst.

The crowd of 9,323 saw Crystal Palace have most of the play without being able to turn their possession to advantage. In the second half they forced 13 corners in total, but City defended resolutely and hung on to win after Duane Darby had given them the lead in the 22nd minute. The Tigers ended a goal drought lasting 301 minutes when Darby scored from close range at the second attempt. After Hateley had flicked on a cross by Mann, Darby had a header touched on to the post by Palace goalkeeper Kevin Miller, but he followed up quickly for the only goal of the night.

Palace manager Steve Coppell graciously observed afterwards: "I have always said that these ties should be played over one leg and this has robbed Hull City of a famous victory and a deserved one." It was only a temporary hiccup from the Tigers' point of view and they duly made sure of their passage into the third round when they went to Selhurst Park for the second leg on September 30.

But Hateley, who was trying to sign former England international David Rocastle on loan from Chelsea in the interim, was without Darby and Mann for the second leg because they had to undergo operations, while Hodges, Rob Dewhurst, Adam Lowthorpe and Kevin Gage were also ruled out, but significantly defender Ian Wright was passed fit. Palace were without David Tuttle, Kevin Muscat, Andy Roberts and Lombardo, but defender Marc Edworthy had recovered from a hamstring injury to play.

The Tigers shocked the 6,407 crowd by again taking the lead when Wright headed in at the far post from a corner in the 29th minute to give his side a two-goal cushion. Palace brought on striker George Ndah as they went all-out for the goals that would get them back into contention and they did score two in the second half. Soon after the resumption Carl Veart equalised on the night from Edworthy's cross and then Ndah made it 2-2 on aggregate with Palace's second after 75 minutes. The saga then went into extra time with City knowing that they would be through on the strength of Wright's away goal if it stayed as it was. It did do, but the Tigers had some anxious moments throughout the 120 minutes, notably when the heroic Steve Wilson could only tip Simon Rodger's cross on to the bar.

City's assistant manager Billy Kirkwood summed it up when he said: "It was fantastic – absolutely unbelievable. We rode our luck over two games, but you have got to expect that against Premiership opposition." The victory gave the Tigers, then 91st out of 92 in the League, the chance to do it again because they received a plum away tie at Newcastle United in the third round, but lost 2-0.

The away-goals ruling again helped the Tigers when they were drawn against Stockport County in the first round of the Coca Cola Cup in 1998-99. The back-cloth to the first leg was that it might be City's last season at Boothferry Park, but they had a job to do in the first leg at Edgeley Park on August 11, 1998. The Tigers were without player-manager Mark Hateley because of a groin strain, while Gregor Rioch and Warren Joyce had thigh injuries that ruled them out, so Neil Mann and Brian McGinty were drafted into the starting line-up. Stockport's manager Gary Megson kept the same side who had won 2-1 at Bradford City on the opening day of the League season after defender Martin McIntosh had recovered from a knee problem.

The 3,134 crowd were amazed by the Tigers' initial approach as they went 2-0 in front after only 16 minutes. David Brown nodded in the first from Jon French's cross after a free-kick by Steve Hawes in the 10th minute and then McGinty nipped in for a second when County defender Colin Woodthorpe was short with his back-pass as he tried to cut out a long ball from David d'Auria. Stockport were back in contention before halftime following a disputed penalty after Neil Whitworth had challenged Chris Byrne heavily. Tony Dinning hit the post with his spot-kick, but Ian Moore reacted quickly to head home. And seven minutes from time County equalised when substitute Paul Cook crossed and Byrne volleyed home.

After the 2-2 draw, both sides lost home games in the League before the second leg at Boothferry Park a week later. City were without French, who had damaged an ankle in the first meeting, while Hateley brought in Ben Morley, Mark Greaves and Mike Edwards instead of Kevin Gage, Mann and Lee Ellington. Stockport made four changes from the first leg with Paul Cook, Jim Gannon, Paul Alsaker and Graham Branch all coming into the starting line-up.

The second leg was always going to be a tense affair for the 3,480 crowd at Boothferry Park and both sides created some good chances. Goalkeeper Steve Wilson was in fine form for City, but it was 0-0 after 90 minutes. Both sides had more chances in extra time, but there were still no goals and for the second succes-sive season the Tigers got through a Coca Cola Cup round on the away-goals rule.

City were drawn against another First Division side, Bolton Wanderers, in the second round, but this time they went out on a 6-3 aggregate. Bolton won 3-1 at home in the first leg and, although the Tigers battled valiantly to get back into contention at Boothferry Park, they eventually lost the second leg 3-2.

Once again the Tigers had produced some memorable moments in cup soccer to make up for their failings at League level and it is a pattern that has punctuated the club's fortunes for much of the 20th century. Success has all too often been fleet-ing and transient because City have never fully realised their potential or lived up to expectations and the fact that they have had so many good times in cup football merely serves to underline their inability to do consistently well during a long period and fulfil the fans' general hopes and ambitions for the club. But without them, there really would have been very little for Hull's soccer public to get too excited about.

Chapter Four

Cup
Controversies

WHILE Hull City can reflect upon causing plenty of cup upsets during their existence, there have been other occasions that have typified their capacity for under-achievement. Too often they have gone so near and yet ended up being so far from even greater cup heroics and there has been one common factor which has dominated such escapades – controversy.

Their greatest runs in the FA Cup have always seem to end in despair coated and clouded in rancour and bitterness. It probably would have nothing to do with Hull City if it were otherwise because such episodes are eerily symptomatic of their inability to go all the way in terms of fulfilling ambitions. Whether it has just been bad luck bound up in controversy is open to debate, but the Tigers have so often missed out in uncanny fashion. It has been as if the fates have been forever amassed against them just when they have been on the threshold of something unexpected in terms of cup achievements that would have really put the club on the soccer map. It merely mirrors their well-charted history of anti-climax, of course.

The trend was set in the 1914-15 season when City reached the quarter-finals of the FA Cup for the first time. At that point, though, it was necessary to progress only to the fourth round to do so: nowadays it is the sixth round unless more and more clubs follow Manchester United's lead and pull out!

The seeds had been sown with complaints about the disputed manner of City's cup exit at Newcastle United in the third round in 1910-11. They lost 3-2 even though Joe Smith was on the mark twice and there were strong feelings that one of Newcastle's goals should have been disallowed for offside. It was more than a little ironic, of course, when the Tigers played two friendlies in five days at home to Grimsby Town in April 1925 as trial games for the possible revision of the offside law!

But on March 6, 1915, the Tigers felt that they had been robbed of a place in the semi-finals for the first time when they were drawn away to First Division Bolton Wanderers. Curiously, it was two penalties by another Joe Smith that caused all their trials and tribulations this time.

City's cup run had been impressive because they had already knocked out one First Division side West Bromwich Albion when they beat them 1-0 at Anlaby Road. A 2-1 home win over non-League Northampton Town followed in the second round and then they beat another Southern League side, Southampton, 4-0 in a replay after a 2-2 draw at the Dell. That took the Tigers into the fourth round – then the last eight – for the first time.

Charles Betts had recovered from a leg injury to take his place in City's line-up and their only other worry had been when goalkeeper Nicholson Hendry fell into a ditch when trying to retrieve his ball in a recreational round of golf during the build-up! Bolton fielded an experienced side – David Stokes was qualifying for his third benefit in 13 seasons with the club – but they were fourth from the bottom of the First Division with a dubious record of having lost more games than anyone else and yet being the sixth-highest scorers.

It led to a high-scoring clash with the Tigers, who were 2-0 in front after just 17 minutes thanks to goals from Charles Deacey and Sammy Stevens. But Wanderers were level by halftime with the ball running kindly for Evan Jones for the equaliser. It was the shape of luck to come, in fact, because referee Sephton awarded Bolton two hotly-disputed penalties early in the second half. In the 46th minute Douglas Morgan was ruled to have fouled Frank Roberts, whose foot "appeared to catch in the turf," however. Smith dispatched that penalty off the inside of a post and two minutes later he made it 4-2 from the spot. This time Deacey challenged Ted Vizard in what was mysteriously described as "a perfectly-legitimate and rather ladylike fashion," but again a penalty was awarded. There was then the scene of "the City players clamouring around the referee and the Bolton players smiling at what they took as a huge joke," while Vizard admitted later that he did not think that it should have been a penalty. But even though William Cameron hit the woodwork for the Tigers and some chances went begging, it finished 4-2 and it was ruefully reported: "It was not the players who decided which of the clubs should reach the semi-finals: it was the referee." And it was of minimal compensation that one Bolton official told his City counterparts afterwards: "You need have no fear about your team holding their own in the First Division." As everyone knows, the Tigers have still to find out…

In 1920-21 City again reached the fourth round of the FA Cup, but again they failed to reach the semi-finals. They beat Bath City 3-0 at home in the first round and then won 2-0 at Crystal Palace before pulling off an unexpected piece of giantkilling to defeat high-riding Burnley 3-0 at Anlaby Road. That earned them a quarter-final at home to another First Division side, Preston North End, and, although it took two meetings for the issue to be settled, the whole affair was for once remarkably clear of controversy. It must have been the exception proving the rule…

The first meeting at Anlaby Road on March 5, 1921, attracted a gate of 30,000, comfortably the lowest of the four quarter-finals, and was a surprisingly low-key affair with no goals. It at least meant that City goalkeeper Billy Mercer had kept four clean sheets out of four in the FA Cup so far that season. The only other notable feature of the afternoon seemed to have been the appearance of a monkey mascot who was clad in a miniature Hull City jersey and pants and sat on one of the crossbars after clambering up a post!

It was also noted that "Preston were very robust in their methods," but there were no specific moments of controversy in either of the two meetings. And when the replay took place in front of a crowd of 32,853 at Deepdale five days later, North End won 1-0 with a 13th-minute goal by former England international Frank Jefferis, while they also hit the woodwork twice. Yet in true tradition there was a lot of discontent and discord among a section of the City fans, but it had nothing to do with events on the pitch. This time they were most unhappy that several hundred of them were unable to see the match unless they had reserved seats tickets because interest in the tie was so high that Preston officials locked the gates an hour before the start.

City's best run in the FA Cup was in the 1929-30 season when they reached the semi-finals. But there was a strong feeling that they would have gone the whole hog and reached Wembley if those fates had not conspired against them. The cup run began with a 4-3 win at Plymouth Argyle in the third round when Stan Alexander hit a hat-trick. The Tigers then beat Blackpool 3-1 at home in the fourth round and progressed to the quarter-finals when they came from behind to win at Manchester City in front of a 61,574 crowd. In the sixth round City drew 1-1 at Newcastle United and won 1-0 back at Anlaby Road in the replay.

That led to a semi-final meeting with Arsenal at Elland Road, Leeds, on March 22, 1930, and more than 20 special trains ferried about 11,000 City fans to the game. A group of Leeds United supporters, in fact, looked after the day's catering for almost 500 of their City counterparts at the city's Anglers' Club. And for a while it looked as if the Tigers would reach Wembley as they faced up to an Arsenal forward-line

Jimmy Howieson, who scored for Hull City against Arsenal in the FA Cup semi-finals in March 1930.

who had cost a total of £30,000. Goals by Jimmy Howieson and Douglas "Dally" Duncan put City in the driving seat, but they were handicapped by injuries to James Walsh, who had been a fitness doubt beforehand after being hurt in a League game against Chelsea a week earlier, and Bert "Paddy" Mills. As a result, David Jack, then the country's costliest player at £10,000, and Cliff Bastin earned the Gunners a replay. After the match the City contingent dined at the Royal Station Hotel in Hull and skipper Matt Bell told the crowds who had amassed outside in Paragon Square: "Only injuries to some of our players prevented us from winning. But I have every

Bill McCracken, Hull City's manager when they reached the FA Cup semi-finals in 1929-30.

confidence that we shall be able to beat the Arsenal in the replay." A controversial moment, though, meant that it was not to be.

Arsenal prepared for the replay, which took place at Villa Park four days later, at Brighton, while the Tigers, who brought in Tommy Bleakley and Phil Cartwright, generally had the local support in Birmingham as well the backing of a band of Hull Kingston Rovers fans who travelled to the tie by special train. But Jack scored the only goal after 11 minutes to send Arsenal into the Final although there were vehement claims from City players and fans that the ball had gone dead from Alec James' pass in the build-up to it. The Tigers' goalkeeper Fred Gibson, however, thought that the goal was legitimate, but that did not prevent further controversy. City centre-half Arthur Childs was sent off by referee Kingscott following a challenge involving James and they were left to try to battle back into the game with ten men.

It was all in vain as Arsenal went on to beat Huddersfield Town 2-0 in the Final, but "Paddy" Mills told me many years later: "As we were

Bert "Paddy" Mills, one of Hull City's FA Cup heroes controversially beaten by Arsenal in 1930.

coming off the field at the end, the referee said:'Never mind, 'Paddy,' there are two good teams in the Final.' I'd never heard anything like it, so I reported it to the manager Bill McCracken when we got back to the dressing-room. He asked if I was sure about what the referee had said and, if so, would I repeat it in front of the directors and the FA. I said I'd tell it to anybody and in the end they suspended the referee

Fans congregate for Hull City's best-ever gate of 55,019 for their FA Cup tie against Manchester United in February 1949. The Tigers were controversially beaten 1-0.

for life." None of it, furthermore, prevented City's chairman Dr Durham Pullan from resigning in protest about the refereeing.

The Tigers did not get even as far as the FA Cup quarter-finals again until the 1948-49 season, but controversy struck again. Their cup run had started quietly with victories over Accrington Stanley and Reading at the second attempt before gaining momentum when they knocked out Blackburn Rovers after extra time, Grimsby Town and Stoke City. They were then drawn at home to FA Cup holders Manchester United and the tie was to attract the biggest attendance in Boothferry Park's history, 55,019. It had all the hallmarks of a titanic cup encounter because the Tigers, guided by player-manager Raich Carter, had won their opening nine games in the old Third Division North and lost only twice in 31 games. United, on the other hand, had scored 21 goals in three previous rounds of the competition and could call upon eight of the players who had won the trophy at Wembley the previous season.

Cup tie fever gripped Hull and City director Stan Kershaw claimed that he had received more than 600 letters to his home seeking tickets for the match. And club president Kenneth Percival added: "We are being snowed under with ticket requests. Thousands of letters have come in and we cannot think of opening them, let alone answering them. They are to be dumped for the time being so that the staff can get on with their important normal routine."

In the end the Tigers made the tie all-ticket after consultations with the police and fixed a crowd limit of 55,000. A total of 5,125 tickets were to go to City Supporters' Club members, of whom there were almost 6,000 in various parts of the East Riding, while 13,750 tickets were allocated to United. The next move was to provide extra public transport – but not for the game itself. It was needed just to deal with the distribution of tickets at Boothferry Park on the Sunday before the tie! Cup interest also extended across the River Humber to Barton-upon-Humber, where there was a meeting to form a sub-section of the Tigers' supporters' club. But it overflowed into the street and the police had to admit people in relays so that they could join up.

On the day of the game one City fan produced 2,000 rosettes, which he made himself in less than a fortnight, and sold them at one shilling for adults and half-price for children. The media interest, meanwhile, stretched to 42 sports writers, 28 photographers, three radio commentators and two separate corps of newsreel operators. The entourage included representatives of the French Press and Danish radio!

The next administrative problem concerned some counterfeit tickets at 2s. 6d. each for the North and East stands, so printers were posted at 30 turnstiles to try to detect them. The forgeries were understood to have emanated from Manchester's Smithfield Market. The overall outcome of it all was that two days before the cup tie a meeting took place between City's board and local businessmen to maximise the attraction of soccer in the city. There was unanimous backing for a project to increase the capacity of Boothferry Park to 80,000. It must have seemed like a good idea at the time…

For the game itself the Tigers were without left-winger Eddie Burbanks, but Jimmy Greenhalgh, Allan Mellor and Viggo Jensen were all available after passing fitness tests. United were without their influential captain Johnny Carey because of an ankle injury, so Johnny Ball played in his first cup tie with only three first-team appearances to his name.

There was a fanfare of trumpets as the teams came out and it was Ball who was involved in the build-up to United's controversial 73rd-minute winner. He cleared off the line as City, who had been handicapped from the first half when goalkeeper Billy Bly broke his nose and Jimmy Greenhalgh aggravated an ankle injury in a clash with Charlie Mitten, pressed for a breakthrough. Ball began a counterattack which resulted in Ronnie Burke finding Scottish international Jimmy Delaney, who was playing against his former Glasgow Celtic teammate Willie Buchan. Delaney knocked the ball forward in an attempt to outpace Allan Mellor, who claimed that it had gone dead as it was pulled back from the byline for Stan Pearson to score from close range. Curiously, United's players were slow to acclaim the goal, but there were few other murmurs of complaint from the City camp, so

Hull City goalkeeper Maurice Swan dives to push away a shot from Chelsea's Eddie McCreadie in their FA Cup tie at Stamford Bridge in March 1966.

Nottingham referee Reg Leafe, a linesman at Wembley for the previous year's FA Cup Final, allowed it to stand and the arguments started to rage.

The Tigers did not reach the sixth round of the FA Cup again until the 1965-66 season when they were enjoying another golden era, but controversy was still round the corner. The cup run again began in subdued fashion with wins over Bradford Park Avenue, then a League club, and non-League Gateshead before bursting into life when City, then in the old Third Division, shocked Southampton and Nottingham Forest. They then avoided a potential soccer banana skin against fellow giantkillers Southport before being drawn away to mighty Chelsea at Stamford Bridge on March 26, 1966.

Chelsea's George Graham goes crashing to the ground as Hull City's Mick Milner (left) and Chris Simpkin concentrate on defence in the FA Cup tie at Stamford Bridge in March 1966.

Hull City skipper Andy Davidson, who was unhappy about some of the decisions that went against them when they faced Chelsea at Stamford Bridge in the FA Cup in March 1966.

City dramatically earned a replay in front of a 46,924 crowd with two late goals by Ken Wagstaff after being 2-0 down when Bobby Tambling and George Graham scored for Chelsea. But it was generally felt that the Tigers might have reached the semi-finals at the first attempt if justice had been done and City skipper Andy Davidson said:"We had two distinct penalties turned down and I still feel the same way about it all. John Boyle handled on the line and Eddie McCreadie tapped Ken Wagstaff's legs and sent him flying. Everything went for

Chelsea and against us, but we still had the pluck to fight back and get a draw. At the same time I don't think we should have been in that position."

The referee concerned was Jack Taylor, who was to take charge of the 1974 World Cup Final between West Germany and Holland, in which he awarded a first-minute penalty. But Ken Houghton, whose header was stopped by Boyle, still shakes his head in disbelief nowadays when asked about the injustices of that tie, while City's players have always been amazed by the number of decisions that seemed to go their way when Mr Taylor refereed one of their League games against Oxford United soon afterwards. Apparently Ron Atkinson, who was then playing for Oxford, repeatedly mentioned it during the game! Whatever the rights and wrongs of it all, Mr Taylor admitted to me on a visit to Boothferry Park many years afterwards that City fans still had not let him forget that cup tie at Chelsea…

The outcome was a different referee, Kevin Howley, for the replay at Boothferry Park five days later. It was delayed because of Chelsea's European commitments and took place on General Election day with 45,328 fans voting to fill Boothferry Park. City fans can reflect on a stunning goal with a long-range drive by Chris Simpkin that kept their hopes alive, but they went down 3-1 as Chelsea, who had the emerging Peter Osgood back in their ranks after he had missed the first tie because of illness, got through with Tambling twice and Graham again on the mark. And Andy Davidson mused: "Chelsea were one of the best sides in the country at the time and when we went there, their manager Tommy Docherty said we were a potential First Division side. We were playing like one at the time and in both games we were the

Hull City's centre-half Mick Milner beats Chelsea's George Graham in the air in the FA Cup replay in front of 45,328 fans at Boothferry Park in March 1966.

better side. Everybody was convinced that we were going to Wembley that year, but Chelsea scored five times against us although there wasn't a good goal among them."

City were still attracting big attendances when they reached the FA Cup quarter-finals again in the 1970-71 season. By this time they were in the old Second Division and Terry Neill had taken over as manager from Cliff Britton, but he could do nothing about overcoming the club's FA Cup hoodoo that seemed to strike just when it mattered most. City had beaten Charlton Athletic, Blackpool and Brentford at home before they were rewarded with another tie at Boothferry Park in the sixth round. First Division Stoke City were the visitors and the game attracted another bumper crowd of 41,452.

The Tigers seemed to have one foot in the semi-finals when Ken Wagstaff nonchalantly beat England goalkeeper Gordon Banks twice in the opening 24 minutes, but it was to be another day of anti-climax. Terry Conroy crucially equalised just before halftime and John Ritchie was on the mark twice for the Potters as they hit back to win 3-2, but their comeback was laced with two hotly-disputed incidents.

The first bit of controversy occurred ten minutes from the end when Stoke's

Hull City's Chris Chilton and Stoke City's Denis Smith in one of their epic tussles during the FA Cup tie at Boothferry Park in March 1971.

Hull City players take a stroll on the beach at Scarborough before their FA Cup tie against Stoke City in March 1971 (left to right): Malcolm Lord, Chris Chilton, Ken Wagstaff, Billy Wilkinson and Chris Simpkin.

winner stemmed from a quickly-taken throw-in that arguably should have been awarded to City. But Conroy whipped in a cross from it, Ritchie headed home and the Tigers were out. And City forward Malcolm Lord reflected: "We were robbed when Stoke's winner followed a throw-in which should have been to us, but one of their players took it, play was allowed to continue and they scored." City half-back Chris Simpkin added: "Roger de Vries gave them the ball for the throw-in. He was a good lad, but he was too nice on this occasion because he should have just got on with it, taken it himself and worried about what might happen later."

It was not the end of the arguing, either. City player-manager Terry Neill went close to earning a replay with a powerful header as his side mounted a determined, late onslaught, but Banks somehow clawed it away one-handed with a typically memorable save. But Simpkin observed: "Terry Neill claimed that the ball was over the line, but it was still a brilliant save by Gordon Banks." The Tigers went on to have one of the most successful seasons in their history, but bad luck had again dogged them at a vital stage of the FA Cup.

Hull City, in fact, have never reached the last eight or even the last four of the FA Cup since March 6, 1971. Perhaps subsequent generations of their players have just assumed that it would be hardly worth the effort in the circumstances because of the predecents set over the years. Perhaps it has all spared the loyal fans further heartache. Perhaps it is understandable. Perhaps it is not surprising. I suppose that some sides have had all the luck – even if it is bad…

Chapter Five

Red Faces

HULL City may have pulled off many cup shocks in their time, but they have been typically guilty of losing to lower-grade opposition themselves. The good has outweighed the bad in terms of giantkilling and being giantkilled, but the Tigers' general capacity for under-achieving has meant they have undergone their fair share of embarrassing moments in cup ties.

The Tigers had a particularly bad time of it in their early forays into the FA Cup, for example. It is fair to say that there was something of a levelling-out process in the formative years of top-flight soccer as everything unfolded, so it may not have been such a disgrace for a League club to go out of the FA Cup to non-League opposition in those days as it has more traditionally meant in the latter part of the 20th century.

City, in fact, went out of the FA Cup to non-League opposition in their first venture into the competition in 1904-05, but it is arguable as to whether they were giantkilled – because they were still a non-League side themselves at the time! They were drawn at home to Northern League side Stockton in the preliminary round on September 17, 1904, and that immediately presented the club, formed three months earlier, with a major problem. They had agreed to share the facilities at the Boulevard, but it was needed for a rugby-league game that day and that took precedence. City, accordingly, forsook home advantage and the tie was switched to Stockton, where a crowd of 20,000 had watched an FA Cup tie against Wolverhampton Wanderers the previous season at their Victoria Ground. But the controversy did not end there.

The game ended 3-3 after City had gone 2-0 ahead and then fallen 3-2 behind by halftime. It seemed that the fact that the Tigers ended up earning a 3-3 draw was too much for the Stockton fans, who expected their side to win at the first time of asking, and it was reported: "There could be no excuse for such a hostile demonstration as greeted City when they were driving from the ground. It started with booing and threats and was followed by a shower of stones and broken crockery. Youngsters who hardly knew a football from a bag of biscuits joined in the assault, but they were not so much to blame as some of their elders, who ought to have known better. Several of the City directors and players had narrow escapes from being hit and a number of ugly-looking missiles, gathered afterwards from the bottom of their wagonette, will serve as reminders of the memorable occasion."

City officials, whose outward journey had been marred when their "somewhat antediluvian saloon" broke down, initially thought of appealing for the replay to take place in Hull, but, because the idea might not have been sanctioned, they decided instead to submit a letter of protest about the demonstration that they had faced. At the same time it was thought that the City party need the support of "the Beverley militia" for the replay, while goalkeeper Jimmy Whitehouse threatened to take "a big gun" with him!

Dr George Lilley, City's vice-chairman, was even more unhappy when he found that Stockton did not pay out gate receipts by cheque because they were a limited company, so he had to carry home the prerequisite half-share of £31. 10s. in a bag. At least everyone was happy with the total receipts of £63 because Middlesbrough were playing Arsenal a few miles down the road on the same day.

The Tigers beat Leicester Fosse 2-0 at the Boulevard in-between, but lost 4-1 in the replay five days later. Stockton were only 1-0 ahead at the interval, but they made no mistake in the second half and City's induction into the FA Cup had proved to be harsh in so many ways. It may have been of little wonder then that, having been accepted into League soccer from the 1905-06 season, they were still shell-shocked enough by the various aspects of that initial experience that they were knocked out by non-League sides twice more in quick succession.

In 1905-06, when they finished fifth in the Second Division in their first season in the Football League, City had a good run in the FA Cup and found themselves playing five games in the qualifying rounds alone. They beat Grimethorpe United 8-1 at home, Denaby United 2-0 away, Leeds City 2-1 away after the two sides had drawn 1-1 and Oldham Athletic 2-1 at home. Having reached the first round proper for the first time, they were drawn at home to Southern League side Reading at Anlaby Road cricket ground on January 13, 1906.

Reading, members of the Southern League since 1894, indulged in some special training at Compton in Berkshire before staying overnight at Hull's Grosvenor Hotel before the game, which was to be kicked off by City's president, Sir Seymour King. Cup rules meant that boys and women were not to be admitted at half-price, as was the case for League matches, while the Newland Orphan Home Band agreed to provide music for the occasion.

Reading, led by England amateur international Herbert Smith, were criticised for "adopting some rough and ready methods" and George Rushton, in particular, was on the receiving end of many of them, but City wasted their chances and lost 1-0 to a goal that stemmed from a hotly-disputed free-kick. Their consolation was that the game attracted a crowd of more than 10,000 and gate receipts of £263 15s.

The strength of the Southern League meant that it might be difficult to decipher who really had been the underdogs and that was probably more blatantly the case the following season when the Tigers joined the FA Cup fray in the first round proper and were drawn away to Tottenham Hotspur. Both sides went away to prepare for the tie on January 12, 1906 – City to Worthing and Spurs to Leigh-on-

Sea. City were given the use of training facilities by the management of Worthing FC and were also invited to attend a coursing match in the area during their build-up, which apparently consisted of sprinting and walking exercises in the main. Curiously, Spurs' England amateur international centre-forward Vivian Woodward stayed behind to train instead of joining his teammates at their pre-match headquarters. The Tigers, meanwhile, moved to London's Charterhouse Hotel on the night before the tie and it was then decided that centre-forward Frank Pearson would be ruled out because of a knee injury.

City chairman Alwyn Smith was a late arrival at the game, which had attracted an estimated 25,000 crowd by the start. But he did not miss any goals because there were none throughout the 90 minutes even though the game was exciting enough. It brought a replay at Anlaby Road football ground five days later with the winners being drawn to travel to either Blackburn Rovers or Manchester City in the second round. By the time that the replay took place, the prospective winners knew that they would be going to Blackburn. Both clubs again went away to the coast for special training before the rematch – City to Hornsea and Spurs to Withernsea.

Estimates vary as to the size of the attendance for the replay, but it was officially given as 15,000 and it included most of the Blackburn team. The game kicked off at 3pm and towards the interval the light was beginning to deteriorate, but there was a lack of goals again and on this occasion there was extra time. Referee Hines allowed only a brief break before it started and even prevented City's players from going to the dressing-room. Bit by bit there was going to be only one winner – the light – and after ten minutes' extra time the game was abandoned as a goalless draw. It came after Mr Hines had missed an accidental incident in which City's Jack McQuillan received a blow in the face from Spurs' Scottish full-back John Watson and it was reported: "The light had now practically gone and quite a weird effect was produced by the spectators striking matches to light their pipes, the lights looking like will-o'-the-wisps."

It was back to the High Road ground four days later amid rumours that Tottenham's directors had paid City £150 in addition to their half-share of the gate for the privilege of staging the replay. As it was, there was a 20,000 crowd with receipts of £750. And the fixture congestion would make most modern-day players complain because in-between City drew 1-1 in a League game at Gainsborough Trinity, after which "the beneficial effects of an electric bath got rid of a good deal of stiffness in their limbs and muscles." Half-backs Davy Gordon and William Robinson were passed fit and Jack McQuillan played despite having just had four teeth removed, while Peter Howe was preferred to George Rushton at centre-forward. Spurs, whose captain Alexander Tait was still playing at the age of 35, were also forced to make changes because of injuries, including one to Woodward.

This time there was an end to the deadlock although City almost took the lead when a shot by Gordon Wright hit the outside of a post. But it was Spurs who scored after 25 minutes through Herbert Chapman, who was to become a more famous name as manager of their North London rivals Arsenal as well as Huddersfield Town. George "Tot" Hedley received a facial injury and in the ensuing goalmouth scramble Herbert Chapman, whose brother Harry was to play for the Tigers from 1911 to 1913 and then become the club's secretary before dying tragically young

after a bout of tuberculosis, scored from close range. Joe "Stanley" Smith grazed the bar with a shot for City soon afterwards, but it was not their day because they squandered some good chances and it was generally agreed that it was their worst display of the three cup ties. At the same time the Spurs fans were unhappy to have a penalty claim rejected after a strong challenge by George Browell on James Reid just before halftime. But Tottenham went through and knocked out Blackburn – also at the third attempt – before losing 4-0 at Notts County.

Whatever the after-effects of losing to two non-League sides in successive seasons, it was to be a long time before City were effectively giantkilled again in the FA Cup – 43 years, in fact. It might have been ominous in the 1949-50 season that it took the Tigers, then establishing themselves as a force in the Second Division, two attempts to get the better of Southport, who were in the lower reaches of the Third Division North, in the third round. After a goalless draw at Southport, City won the replay 5-0 with goals by Norman Moore, Don Revie, Ken Harrison, Eddie Burbanks and Jimmy Greenhalgh and it earned them a visit to another Third Division North side, Stockport County, in the fourth round on January 28, 1950.

Stockport had already knocked out another Second Division side, Barnsley, in the third round and they had an impressive home record at Edgeley Park, which hosted a crowd of 26,600 for the clash with the Tigers, whose player-manager Raich Carter maintained the strategy of playing himself on the left-wing. The tie was special for former City half-back Billy Newton, who was then County's long-serving trainer, and there were 52,000 applications for tickets, which meant that some were selling at double their cost price on the black market outside the ground.

Hull City in 1950-51. Back row (left to right): Don Revie, Alec Gibson, Billy Bly, Tom Berry, Denis Durham; front row: Ken Harrison, Fred Smith, Gerry Bowler, Bobby Gibson, Jimmy Greenhalgh, Alec Bloxham.

Hull City player-manager Raich Carter.

For the second round in succession City had to settle for a goalless draw on a trip to a Third Division North side and it was agreed that on the hard ground they owed much to what was called their BBC combination – Billy Bly in goal, centre-half Gerry Bowler and Raich Carter in the forward-line. For the replay, Burbanks was fit to return in place of Revie, while Greenhalgh, Moore and Viggo Jensen all recovered from knocks to play. But 39-year-old Alec Herd was the architect of a shock 2-0 victory for County, scoring the first goal himself after 33 minutes, and City's long run of avoiding FA Cup embarrassment was over. Stockport had earned themselves a plum fifth-round tie at home to Liverpool, but they lost 2-1. It was, however, the start of three FA Cup exits in four seasons against lower-grade opposition for the Tigers.

In 1950-51 City started their FA Cup run as giantkillers and ended it by being giantkilled. They beat First Division Everton 2-0 at home with goals by Raich Carter and Syd Gerrie in the third round and then defeated the future Third Division North champions Rotherham United in the fourth. Again it was a 2-0 victory at Boothferry Park and Carter and Ken Harrison were on the mark. It brought the Tigers a fifth-round trip to Third Division South side Bristol Rovers, who had been unbeaten at home so far that season, on February 10, 1951.

But they were not at full strength for the game because their new record signing England international centre-half Neil Franklin, who had cost £22,500 from Stoke City after long, drawn-out talks and arrived at Boothferry Park via Colombian side Santa Fe, was ineligible. Harold Meens returned at centre-half in the absence of Franklin and Tom Berry, while inside-forward Syd Gerrie was also injured. As a result, Viggo Jensen went into the forward-line with John Varney taking over at left-back. Bristol Rovers were without their potential match-winner George Petherbridge, who had a pulled muscle, but they hardly missed him.

The crowd of 30,724 saw Rovers gain the upper hand and go into the lead after 28 minutes when John Watling scored from ten yards out at the second attempt. City were forced into a reshuffle when Jensen suffered a head wound, but they continued to struggle in the muddy conditions and Rovers went through thanks to an emphatic 3-0 victory. In the second half Watling grabbed his second goal and then Vic Lambden completed the scoring as Rovers earned themselves a meeting with Newcastle United, the eventual winners, in the quarter-finals.

Two seasons later City produced an FA Cup action replay when they started the competition as giantkillers and ended it by being giantkilled. In the third round they beat First Division Charlton Athletic 3-1 at Boothferry Park with goals by Ken Horton, Viggo Jensen and Bill Harris on January 10, 1953, so the prospect of entertaining Gateshead, from the Third Division North, three weeks later should hardly have brought them out in a collective rash at the thought of it. But Gateshead had indulged in a spot of giantkilling of their own in the third round by knocking out Liverpool and they were at full strength for the clash with City after completing their preparations for it at Hornsea. The Tigers, for their part, included Frank Harrison at centre-half because Tom Berry had a foot injury, while Viggo Jensen reverted to left-back with Paul Todd slotting in at inside-left.

The tie attracted a gate of 37,063, but a gale-force wind made conditions unattractive and City were soon on the defensive as all the goals came in the first half. It took Gateshead only four minutes to go ahead, in fact, when Johnny Ingham scored from close range after City had failed to clear a corner. Ernie Phillips, who had almost given the Tigers the lead after just 15 seconds when the wind caught his long clearance, then turned another shot by Ingham into his own goal to give Gateshead a 2-0 cushion. City plugged away to get back into the game, mainly thanks to left-winger Brian Cripsey's promptings, but all they had to show for it was a goal by Syd Gerrie as they went down 2-1 and lost to lower-grade opponents in the FA Cup for the third time in four seasons.

It was not until November 25, 1961, that the Tigers, by then a mid-table Third Division side, were to suffer further FA Cup humiliation. They defeated non-League Rhyl 5-0 in the first round with goals by Chris Chilton (two), John McSeveney, Ray

Henderson and Eric McMillan and were then given an thoroughly intriguing tie to contemplate. Early in the close season of 1961 manager Bob Brocklebank, who had marched City to promotion in 1959 and then marched them down again a year later, resigned and almost immediately found himself another job when he signed a three-year contract to take charge of Bradford City. Cliff Britton was his successor at Boothferry Park and fate was to dictate that the Tigers should be drawn at home to Brocklebank's Bradford City, who were becoming a force in the Fourth Division, in the second round.

City kept the same side who had won 2-0 in the League at Newport County, while Bradford brought in winger Derek Hawksworth as the replacement for Trevor Hockey, who had joined Nottingham Forest in a £15,000 deal in midweek. And both sides wore change strips with City in all-white and Bradford in royal blue. But the Tigers never rose to the occasion and goalkeeper Bernard Fisher had an unhappy afternoon – an ironic factor because he was to move to Bradford City in the summer of 1963. He missed the ball as he dived to try to save David "Bronco" Layne's shot for the opening goal after 21 minutes and then he allowed Bobby Webb to beat him to the ball for the second on the hour as City slumped to a 2-0 defeat. Bob Brocklebank had got his revenge and Cliff Britton was left to admit: "We cannot quibble. On the day we were beaten by a better side."

Three years later the Tigers, still in the Third Division, were to go out of the FA Cup to Lincoln City, who were embarking on their way to becoming their bogey side. In the first round City had won 4-1 at non-League Kidderminster Harriers when goals by Billy Wilkinson (two), John McSeveney and Terry Heath saw them safely through. But on December 5, 1964, they faced the Imps, who had to apply for re-election to the Fourth Division at the end of the season, in the second round at Boothferry Park in front of a 10,167 gate. City were unchanged after clearing up fitness doubts about Dennis Butler, who had had knee trouble, and Chris Chilton, who had had a thigh problem. Lincoln, who prepared for the tie at Skegness,

Gerry Summers, who scored for Hull City in the FA Cup against Lincoln City in December 1964.

brought back Brian "Bud" Houghton at centre-forward because Bernard "Bunny" Larkin had been injured in training.

It was Houghton who put Lincoln ahead after 35 minutes before Gerry Summers scored a rare goal to equalise for the Tigers seven minutes later. It was to stay 1-1 even though City mounted an amazing onslaught in which Lincoln goalkeeper Malcolm White, who had apparently complained that he had been fouled in the build-up to the equaliser, some-how kept his side in contention with a series of extremely unorthodox and downright fortunate saves, several of them with his legs. It was, therefore, a classic piece of litotes when the Imps' manager Bill Anderson said afterwards: "I was glad when the final whistle went."

Four days later the Tigers went to Sincil Bank for the replay with a third-round trip to Rotherham United awaiting the winners and paid a harsh penalty for failing to take their chances in the first meeting. After clearing up injury doubts about Summers, who had had a damaged calf muscle, and Ken Wagstaff, who had taken a knock on his ankle, City manager Cliff Britton made two changes, recalling Doug Clarke and Ray Henderson in place of Wilkinson and Heath. Lincoln were unchanged and again went away to Skegness to prepare for the game.

If Malcolm White had been the Imps' hero in the first meeting, then City's goalkeeper Maurice Swan was regarded as their villain in the replay. Early in the second half the Imps gained the initiative with a two-goal lead when Swan failed to cling on to shots by winger Ken Fencott, who scored himself eight minutes after "Bud" Houghton had snapped up the rebound from the first in the 47th minute. What made it more annoying for the Tigers was that Lincoln took the lead when they were temporarily down to ten men as inside-right John Milner received attention to a head injury. McSeveney gave City some hope when he reduced the arrears 20 minutes from time, but in the final minute Milner gave the Imps a 3-1 win when he restored their two-goal advantage.

The Tigers' next FA Cup disgrace did not occur until the 1976-77 season, but again they went of the competition in a replay after they had originally been drawn at home to Port Vale in the third round. City were in mid-table security in the old Second Division at the time, while Vale were to avoid relegation from the Third Division by only three points that season. But there were doubts as to whether the tie would even go ahead on January 8, 1977, because of the cold weather. City put a large gas heater and some coconut matting down on the Boothferry Park pitch on the night before the game, but even then it took three inspections by referee Keith Styles before he passed it fit for play.

City waited to check on the condition of the pitch before deciding whether captain Billy Bremner was able to return after an ankle injury, but he passed a fitness test, so Paul Haigh moved back into defence at the expense of Ian Dobson. In addition, Dave Stewart played his first senior game for a little more than three months because Dave "Kipper" Gibson had a leg injury. Vale included teenage goalkeeper Trevor Dance in place of the injured John Connaughton and were without the suspended Colin Tartt.

The Tigers failed to make the most of the chances that fell to them and the tie did not really come alive for the 9,694 spectators until the closing stages. Vale were reduced to ten men while they hesitated over a substitution and City midfield player Gordon Nisbet broke the deadlock with his

Hull City's popular defender Gordon Nisbet, who scored his first goal for the club in an FA Cup tie at home to Port Vale in January 1977.

Hull City's former Scottish international captain Billy Bremner, who was hurt in an off-the-ball incident in an FA Cup tie at Port Vale in January 1977.

first goal for the club when he scrambled the ball home following Bremner's free-kick with four minutes remaining. But then in the final minute the Tigers claimed that they should had a free-kick for a foul on goalkeeper Jeff Wealands by David Harris as Vale made it 1-1 with an equaliser from Ken Beamish.

The replay for the right to entertain either Lincoln City or Burnley in the fourth round took place at Vale Park two days later and the Tigers brought back striker Jeff Hemmerman because John Hawley had damaged knee ligaments in the first meeting. Dobson was brought into the defence to enable Haigh to replace Dave Stewart, while Wealands had to have a check on an eye injury that he had suffered in the incident leading up to Vale's equaliser. The Valiants brought in striker Ray Williams in place of winger Ken Beech.

City were beginning to enter an annoying phase of giving away crucial late goals and they did so for the fourth time in six games to take the replay into extra time, but there was plenty of controversy before that occurred. The Tigers felt that they should have had a penalty when John Ridley handled and that Ken Beamish should have been dismissed for elbowing Bremner off the ball. It merely added to their frustrations when Beamish scored twice during the evening: in fact, he almost gave Vale the lead in the first half when he hit the post. City, on the other hand, hit the woodwork twice in normal time thanks to George Lyall and Jeff Hemmerman. But it was again 1-1 after 90 minutes with City again taking the lead and then throwing it away late on. They got the breakthrough after 57 minutes when Lyall's corner was not properly cleared and Hemmerman scored at the second attempt. But five minutes from the end Vale were level when Beamish struck with a shot from the edge of the penalty area.

Vale took command for the first time in extra time and went ahead in the 101st minute when Beech took a flick from Williams and set up the chance for Kevin Kennerley to score with a dipping shot from 20 yards. As City desperately chased the game, the Valiants increased their lead three minutes from the end of extra time to secure a 3-1 victory in front of 10,668 fans. Again it was Beamish who did the damage when he rose to head home from a corner by Terry Bailey.

City fans had by that time seen any FA Cup defeat as a watershed in the club's season. That was because the Tigers were invariably stuck in the mid-table comfort zone in the old Second Division and the FA Cup in particular brought them badly-needed hope of something a little more exciting in their lives. They were unhappy about the defeat and City manager John Kaye insisted defiantly: "I have no comment to make to the fans because the lads played well as far as I'm concerned. It is just a lack of know-how when it comes to finishing off. We are snapping at everything in order to be sure when good concentration is what is really needed." Kaye was always honest and down-to-earth, so it was a little out of character when he added that, despite their defeat, City had played Vale off the park. The comment was almost a precursor to England cricket coach David Lloyd's famed "We murdered them" epithet in similarly defiant circumstances on a visit to Zimbabwe more recently. As it was, City chairman Christopher Needler gave Kaye a vote of confidence – and he did actually survive for a further nine months.

It was another ten years before the Tigers, again a mid-table Second Division outfit, were to be giantkilled again in the FA Cup. In 1986-87 they had high hopes of earning a place in the quarter-finals despite receiving three successive away draws. They had won 2-1 at Shrewsbury Town in the third round with goals by Frank Bunn and Andy Saville and then beaten Swansea City 1-0 at Vetch Field when Richard Jobson scored the winner. It meant that a fifth-round trip to Wigan Athletic, who were to reach the Play-offs in the Third Division that season, on February 21, 1987, held out plenty of promise even though they had lost only one cup tie at Springfield Park in 20 years.

The Tigers, who prepared for the tie at Keele University, were without the suspended Pat Heard and Bunn, who had been sent off in the fourth-round win at Swansea, while Peter Skipper, Garreth Roberts and Saville all required late fitness tests before being able to play because of ankle, hamstring and back problems respectively. Wigan's centre-back Andy Holden had recovered from a groin strain, while winger Ian Griffiths took over from Paul Cook.

As had been the case at Port Vale ten years earlier, City dominated the game, failed to take their chances and slipped to an ignominious defeat. Wigan ended the stalemate after 58 minutes when Chris Thompson put them ahead from David Lowe's pass and two more goals gave them a clear-cut 3-0 triumph in front of a crowd of 11,453. They added a second after 78 minutes when Paul Jewell, more recently Bradford City's successful manager, scored after Lowe's shot had been blocked and Bobby Campbell completed the scoring five minutes later.

City manager Brian Horton, equally as candid and single-minded as John Kaye had been ten years earlier, admitted that he had made a mistake when he substituted Billy Askew shortly before the Latics' second goal. And just like Kaye, he struggled to accept that his side had been giantkilled after dominating a tie so much because he said:"I can't believe we lost 3-0, but we've got to pick ourselves up and lift our heads. Perhaps with a bit more belief in ourselves, it might have been us going through, but good luck to Wigan."

Hull City's long-serving Billy Askew, who was surprisingly substituted in an FA Cup tie at Wigan Athletic in February 1987.

City's naughty 1990s, during which their fortunes have repeatedly slipped to an all-time low, have brought them three forgettable FA Cup episodes, starting with the 1993-94 season when they were in the Second Division. There was something ominous about the start of their FA Cup involvement because they were leading 1-0 at non-League Runcorn when a wall inside the ground collapsed and their first-round tie was abandoned. But at the second time of asking they got through with Linton Brown and Chris Hargreaves scoring in a 2-0 triumph and that earned them a second-round visit to Chester City at the Deva Stadium on December 4, 1993. City chairman Martin Fish and manager Terry Dolan were already looking forward to a money-spinning third-round tie because of the club's financial worries, but Chester, who were to achieve automatic promotion from the Third Division as runners-up that season, had to be overcome first.

City brought back former England under-21 international striker Steve Moran and switched Graeme Atkinson to a defensive role with David Mail being relegated to the substitutes' bench. Chester recalled leading marksman Stuart Rimmer and skipper Chris Lightfoot was able to play despite having had eight stitches in a facial wound. David Pugh also passed a late fitness check, but David Thompson was ruled out. Paul Wheeler, who had had a brief spell with the Tigers during the 1989-90 season, faced his old club.

Chester pulled off an upset in front of 4,333 fans because they took their chances better than City, who, however, were unlucky when Greg Abbott and Chris Hargeaves both hit the woodwork. Chester went ahead after just eight minutes when defender Roger Preece scored his first goal for the club with a shot that flew past startled City goalkeeper Alan Fettis. And in the 32nd minute they increased their lead when another defender, Colin Greenall, headed home from Chris Lightfoot's corner. It finished 2-0 although Chester hardly got a money-spinning third-round tie themselves – an away trip to Plymouth Argyle – but at least they had got through.

The Tigers still desperately needed a major influx of cash the following season when the FA Cup came round and chairman Martin Fish and manager Terry Dolan promised supporters during the build-up to the club's first-round tie at home to Third Division Lincoln City on November 12, 1994, that they would not sell striker Dean Windass for less then £500,000. City brought back leading goalscorer Linton Brown in place of Chris Hargreaves, while Lincoln's manager Sam Ellis opted for an experienced line-up as he recalled Steve Foley and Trevor Hebberd in midfield and Gary Bannister up front. Matt Carbon was preferred to David Johnson, but Ellis was unable to call upon loan signings Russell Hoult and Richard Lucas.

The Tigers, watched by a crowd of just 5,758, continued their pattern of going out of the FA Cup in distressing circumstances because they had squandered a succession of chances with Windass having an off-day. The Imps, whose side included Colin Greenall from Chester's giantkillers the previous season, defended in numbers and, as is so often the case in soccer, punished City by scoring from one of the few opportunities that they created. The only goal of the game came in the 53rd minute when City defender Rob Dewhurst slipped as he tried to clear the ball and Dean West set up a neatly-taken winner for Gary Bannister.

Worse was to follow, though, on November 15, 1997, when the Tigers faced non-League opposition in the first round of the FA Cup. They were drawn at home to

GM Vauxhall Conference side Hednesford Town, who had started to make a name for themselves thanks to their FA Cup exploits and were able to boast an experienced squad by non-League standards. The national media, in fact, took a major interest in the tie largely because they were anticipating an upset.

City's player-manager Mark Hateley was still sidelined because of an Achilles tendon problem, but defender Kevin Gage returned after an ankle injury and Neil Mann and Duane Darby were back in first-team action for the first time for two months. Former England international David "Rocky" Rocastle and Chris Bettney were ineligible as loan signings, while Hednesford did include a one-time international midfield player, Robbie Dennison, who had played for Northern Ireland after making his name with Wolverhampton Wanderers.

The game was to become a tale of two penalties – one that was given and one that was not allowed – and Whitley Bay referee David Laws tellingly said afterwards that it would be "inappropriate to comment" on his controversial decisions. Many of the 6,091 fans at the game gave him a rough ride and City defender Gregor Rioch, who had been sent off by Mr Laws in a Third Division game against Swansea City earlier in the season, was on the receiving end of both hotly-disputed incidents. After 37 minutes Rioch was ruled to have brought down Carl Beeston, who made the most of a fairly-innocuous challenge, and Mr Laws gave a penalty, from which Mick Norbury, who had made his name as a goalscorer in non-League soccer in East Yorkshire with Bridlington Town, scored. Matt Hocking and Duane Darby both hit the woodwork as City retaliated, but the writing was on the wall towards the end when Rioch appeared to be body-checked by Hednesford's defender Kevin Collins as he made a surging run across the box and this time Mr Laws rejected the penalty appeals. And as the Tigers chased the game, Town caught them on the break in the final minute when Joe O'Connor dashed way to seal a 2-0 win.

City had gone out of the FA Cup to a non-League side for the first time since January 1907 and there were some bitter recriminations from their camp towards referee Laws with regard to the manner

Hull City's Gregor Rioch, who was involved in penalty controversies during the FA Cup exit against non-League Hednesford Town at Boothferry Park in November 1997.

Hull-born Alan Hardaker, who did much to foster the Football League Cup.

of their exit. Hateley insisted: "The man in the middle created absolute chaos and he basically lost control of the game." And City chairman David Lloyd said of Hednesford's opening goal: "Luck plays an enormous part in sport and if that was a penalty, I'm a Dutchman." Presumably his international tennis contemporary Tom Okker would be fascinated by the notion...

The advent of the Football League Cup in 1960 gave League clubs extra scope for success each season and it was six years before Hull City came a cropper in it against lower-division opposition. The competition was regarded as the brainchild of League secretary Alan Hardaker, who was born in Hull and played for City's reserves as a half-back, eventually rejecting the chance to turn professional with the club. Hardaker, whose brother Ernest was a long-serving Hull FC supremo, joined the Football League as their assistant secretary in 1951 after spells as a civil servant in his home city and Portsmouth and became their secretary six years later. In 1979 he became the League's director-general, but died at the age of 67 the following year. The late Bill Mallinson, who worked for the Daily Mail, always used to complain gleefully when, as he put it, Alan Hardaker's local club Hull City used to turn their backs on the competition that he had instigated…

Hull City's goal-keeper Maurice Swan, who was dogged by injury in the Football League Cup against Lincoln City in August 1966.

In 1966-67 the Tigers were new to the old Second Division after a memorable promotion campaign, but their planning had gone slightly awry and they were caught out when they were drawn away to Lincoln City, who were to finish at the bottom of the Fourth Division that season, in the first round of the League Cup. City's only experienced goalkeeper Maurice Swan had missed the opening League game of the season at Coventry because of a thigh injury, so Ian McKechnie, who had been freed by Southend United, had been signed on a month's trial. But McKechnie was ineligible for the cup tie, so Swan was patched up and had to play. It was the Tigers' only change to their line-up, but it rebounded on them against an unchanged Lincoln side on August 24, 1966, in a tie watched by a crowd of 6,238.

The Imps took the lead after 27 minutes when the unmarked Joe Bonson headed in a cross from Geoff Smith and City were repeatedly denied by goalkeeper Colin Treharne as they fought back. Chris Simpkin hit the post, referee Harold Davey blocked a shot by Chris Chilton and there was no more scoring. All along, though, Swan was struggling because he used his damaged right leg to kick the ball only once before his teammates had to help him out, he had his thigh heavily strapped up at halftime and 15 minutes from time he crumpled to the ground near a post and had to be substituted. It meant that as the Tigers mounted one final onslaught, they had to reshuffle their side with Dennis Butler taking over in goal, Ken Houghton going to left-back and substitute Terry Heath joining the forward-line. But the end-product was an inauspicious defeat.

Two seasons later City again went out of the League Cup to a Fourth Division outfit when they were drawn away to Brentford, one of the early-season pacesetters, in the second round on September 4, 1968. The Tigers had already defeated Halifax Town, who were not far behind the Bees in the League table, 3-0 in the first round when Ken Wagstaff, Billy Wilkinson and Chris Chilton were on the mark at the Shay. In addition, City had not lost to Brentford in 17 meetings, but all good things came to an end on this occasion.

Wagstaff had scored four times on his last trip to Griffin Park with City, but this time he had two efforts disallowed for offside, other chances went begging and Brentford made the most of some defensive lapses. They took the lead after only eight minutes when George Dobson intercepted a pass by Tom Wilson and sent Allan Mansley through a gap to score and 28 minutes later they added a second when Bobby Ross nodded on John Richardson's long throw and Ronnie Fenton darted in to head home. After 53 minutes the Bees completed a 3-0 win in front of 11,480 fans when a pass by Simpkin went astray and Mansley sped away for his second goal of a night of shocks round the country in the competition.

In 1975-76 City produced a giantkilling act in one Yorkshire derby in the Football League Cup and then were on the receiving of one in another. They accounted for Preston North End and then Yorkshire rivals Sheffield United, who were then in the First Division, before being drawn at Doncaster Rovers, who were sixth in the Fourth Division at the time, in the third round on November 11, 1975. The Tigers had several long-term injury absentees, so they were relieved that Stuart Croft and Ken Wagstaff came through late fitness checks satisfactorily, while Alf Wood and John Hawley were recalled to the starting line-up instead of youngsters Dave Gibson and Dave Stewart. Rovers' manager Stan Anderson named an unchanged side.

The tie attracted an excellent gate of 20,476 and it was certainly not one of those occasions when City were too complacent. Rovers struggled to contain left-winger Roy Greenwood and the Tigers created a host of good chances, but they frustratingly missed one after another with Wood the main culprit. Wood did score in the 31st minute when he volleyed home after a build-up involving Wagstaff, Chris Galvin, Greenwood and Hawley, but it was an equaliser because Doncaster had gone ahead after ten minutes when Freddie Robinson took Chris Balderstone's quickly-taken free-kick and crossed for Brendan O'Callaghan to set up a goal for Peter Kitchen. Rovers regained the lead after 68 minutes when Ray Ternent, whose brother Stan was to become City's manager in 1989, headed home O'Callaghan's cross via a post and it stayed 2-1 even though the unlucky Wood had a second equaliser disallowed.

The Tigers had been linked with a further move for England international Alan Ball and a player-exchange deal had been mentioned with Arsenal, whose manager Bertie Mee was at the cup tie to watch John Hawley. Nothing materialised, however, even though Hawley did end up at Highbury by a more circuitous route almost six years later. And City manager John Kaye was left to muse: "I'd rather have had Doncaster's chances and won. But if we'd taken 25 per cent of ours, we would have won."

It was Lincoln City revisited for the Tigers in 1980-81 and another upset at the hands of the club who have humiliated them most in cup ties. Mike Smith was starting his first full season in charge of Third Division City and brought in former Welsh international defender John Roberts for his debut after signing him for £17,500 from Wrexham. He replaced Dale Roberts, who had a broken nose, while Micky Horswill and Nick Deacy were also ruled out by injuries. But Dennis Booth, who was facing one of his old clubs, and Garreth Roberts passed late fitness tests. Lincoln manager Colin Murphy was without striker Gordon Hobson because of damaged ankle ligaments, but he included close-season signings Colin Boulton and Steve Thompson.

The first leg at Sincil Bank was watched by a crowd of 3,538 on August 9, 1980, and John Roberts was booked in the first minute of his City debut. It was still 0-0 at halftime, but the second half was to prove disastrous for the Tigers as the Imps scored five times with Mick Harford grabbing a hat-trick. He opened the scoring after 47 minutes after Tony Norman had parried a shot by Tony Cunningham, who set up the second for Derek Bell after 61 minutes after he had robbed John Roberts. Harford side-footed home the third goal ten minutes later and completed his hat-trick in the 80th minute when he volleyed in Trevor Thompson's centre. It became 5-0 a minute from time when Cunningham and Trevor Thompson created a goal for George Shipley.

Mike Smith apologised for his side's display, saying: "It got to the stage that Lincoln looked as though they were going to score every time they went forward. It was one of those nightmares. We tried to play an offside trap that we had never talked about. It was unbelievable – we were appealing from the halfway line." Not surprisingly, the second leg three days later did not appeal to many folk. Only 2,933 spectators turned up to Boothferry Park for what was nothing more than an academic occasion. Smith made two changes, bringing in Micky Horswill and Rob McDonald, who had been on loan to Dutch club SC Cambuur, instead of Steve Richards and Brian Marwood, while Lincoln were unchanged.

Again it was 0-0 at halftime and again Harford did the damage in the second half with two more goals. After 54 minutes he picked up John Roberts' clearance and sidestepped Gordon Nisbet and Paul Haigh to score and 18 minutes later he seized on an error by Paul Moss and exchanged passes with Cunningham for his second. It finished up 2-0 on the night and 7-0 on aggregate – and it might have been have been worse because Norman saved a last-minute penalty by Cunningham, who had been pushed by Nisbet.

There was an action replay in 1989-90 when the Tigers went out of what was by then the Littlewood's Cup to Fourth Division opposition from Lincolnshire. City, however, were in the Second Division and their giantkillers were Grimsby Town. And it was probably a bigger shock than usual because the Tigers finished the first leg at Boothferry Park on August 22, 1989, in front. City manager Colin Appleton, who had once had an 18-month spell as the Mariners' coach, was without Neil Buckley because of illness and Ken de Mange and Garreth Roberts because of injuries. Town's manager Alan Buckley also had injury problems and was without John McDermott and John Cockerill, more recently his No. 2 at Blundell Park, but his close-season signing Garry Birtles, the former England striker, had recovered from hamstring trouble to go on to the substitutes' bench.

The 5,045 crowd saw City win 1-0 and only some fine saves by Town's goalkeeper Steve Sherwood prevented the winning margin from being greater. The Tigers were ahead after just 15 minutes when Wayne Jacobs set up a chance for Keith Edwards, whose drive was pushed out by Sherwood for Andy Payton to score from the rebound. It was largely one-way traffic after that, but City were unable to capitalise further on their superiority and it was a factor that was to come back and haunt them.

A week later the action switched to Blundell Park, where there was a crowd of 6,758. There were changes from the first meeting because Appleton dropped Peter Swan, who had had a slight hamstring problem, and Edwards to the substitutes' bench with Nicky Brown and Leigh Jenkinson taking their places, while goalkeeper Iain Hesford was ruled out because of a back injury, so his transfer-listed deputy

Gavin Kelly took over. Strangely, Sherwood was missing because of back trouble, so Paul Reece replaced him, but Cockerill was back in action at the expense of Tommy Watson, who later had a loan spell with the Tigers.

The scores were level on aggregate after just seven minutes when the ball broke off Town's striker Keith Alexander and spun into the net after Tony Rees had instigated the move. That was how it stayed until extra time and Kelly produced some important saves to keep the Tigers in contention. They had a let-off in the 109th minute when Gary Childs hit the bar, but two minutes from the end of extra time he made no mistake when he curled home a shot from just outside the penalty box to see Town through.

Scarborough were to finish in a perilous 23rd position in the Third Division in 1994-95, but it did not stop them from ousting the Tigers from the Coca Cola Cup in the first round that season. City were reeling from a 4-0 defeat at Oxford United in the Second Division as they prepared for the first leg at Boothferry Park on August 16, 1994, and there were recalls for Gary Hobson and Linton Brown instead of Neil Allison and Chris Hargreaves. Scarborough's new manager Billy Ayre included four ex-Tigers in his starting line-up – Gavin Kelly, Mark Calvert, Gary Swann and Stuart Young.

The meagre crowd of 2,546 were happy early on as the Tigers dominated the first half and took a 27th-minute lead when Richard Peacock took Brown's pass, beat Steve Charles and scored with a firm drive. Four minutes later City lost skipper Greg Abbott with a groin strain, but they increased their lead after 64 minutes when Chris Lee flicked home substitute Neil Mann's near-post corner to score against his old club. But the two-goal lead was short-lived because two minutes later 'Boro' crucially made it 2-1 as Ian Blackstone took advantage of an error by Simon Dakin to cross for Young to score with a superb header.

That meant that Scarborough needed only a 1-0 win in the second leg at Seamer Road to go through: as it was, they did twice as well as that. What made matters worse was that even though the tie attracted only 2,287 spectators, there was a lot of crowd trouble involving City followers. The Tigers had Adam Lowthorpe, Mann and Hargreaves in their starting line-up in comparison with the first leg, while 'Boro' had a new strike force of Darren Foreman and Jason White.

The Tigers soon fell behind when Blackstone scored after goalkeeper Alan Fettis had blocked a shot by Foreman, but 'Boro' were reduced to ten men after only 21 minutes when Darren Knowles was dismissed for bringing down Mann in full flight. City could not take advantage of that piece of good fortune, though, and the nearest that they came to scoring was when Hargreaves hit the post. Scarborough, in contrast, saved themselves the onus of extra time when they went through on a 3-2 aggregate after Blackstone had cleverly lobbed home his second goal in the 67th minute.

That embarrassing exit against Scarborough was typical of a lot of City's cup efforts during the club's slump of the 1990s because they developed a depressingly-consistent habit of going out of what had originally been the Associate Members' Cup to lower-division sides. The competition kept reappearing in different guises depending on who could be persuaded to sponsor it and even though it was not the most important item on the soccer calendar, it did represent a road to Wembley – with big financial bonuses in the later stages – after its inaugural season.

The Tigers' difficulties with the competition, though, had started when it was called the Freight Rover Trophy in 1984-85 and they went out of it to Fourth Division Mansfield Town. City were promoted from the Third Division that season, but they still suffered some cup indignity after drawing the first leg at Boothferry Park 2-2 when Colin Calderwood, later a Scottish international, put through his own goal and Billy Whitehurst was also on the mark. Neil Whatmore and Tony Lowery were the Stags' goalscorers and Lowery scored again in the second leg. Noel Luke was Mansfield's other marksman in a 2-1 win that sent City, for whom Billy Askew was on target, out on a 4-3 aggregate.

That exit was a prelude to a far worse sequence in the tournament in the 1990s because the Tigers suffered went out of it in injudicious circumstances for four successive seasons under Terry Dolan's management. On the first three occasions the competition was known as the Autoglass Trophy and City's troubles began in 1991-92. They reached the quarter-finals as a Third Division club before losing 1-0 at Gresty Road on February 4, 1992, to Crewe Alexandra, who were en route to a place in the Fourth Division Play-offs, as Tony Naylor scored the winner.

The following season City, who were in what was the new Second Division, reached the second round before losing 1-0 at Boothferry Park to Chesterfield, who were then a mid-table Third Division side, as Trevor Hebberd snatched the only goal of the game. The format changed to a round-robin system in the first round in 1993-94, but the Tigers fared no better. The name was changed to the Auto Windscreens Shield in 1994-95, but still the Tigers fared no better. They remained in the Second Division, but failed to beat Third Division opposition in four matches and went out at the first stage of the competition.

City drew 1-1 at Scunthorpe United on October 19, 1993, Greg Abbott putting them in front with a diving header before Matt Carmichael equalised. They then ensured that they went out of the competition on November 9 with a 2-0 defeat at home to Scarborough, for whom ex-Tiger Mark Calvert and Darren Davis were on the mark. The following season City went out after losing twice to Third Division sides. On September 27, 1994, Doncaster Rovers beat them 2-0 at Boothferry Park with goals by Lee Thew and Graeme Jones and on November 8 their bogey side Lincoln City defeated them 1-0 at Sincil Bank with a goal by Dean West. Whatever the competition, therefore, the Tigers were capable of providing disappointments for their long-suffering supporters.

Chapter Six

Close Ties

HULL City might have had their moments of FA Cup shame when they went out of the competition to lower-grade opposition, but for a long while they avoided the ultimate ignominy – losing to a non-League club. There may have been some mitigation for going out to two strong Southern League clubs, Reading and Tottenham Hotspur, as the structure of English soccer was still evolving in the early part of the 20th century. Going out to GM Vauxhall Conference side Hednesford Town towards the end of the century might be less excusable, though. It still should not happen even though the Football Conference have slowly earned a reputation as a kind of unofficial fifth division of the Football League and more and more of their sides are going full-time.

But some League clubs have been unceremoniously dumped out of the FA Cup by non-League opposition with remarkable regularity as the gap has slowly closed between the respective standards. Sides have a better chance of avoiding such mishaps, of course, if they are in the top two divisions of English soccer and do not enter the competition until the third round when the threat from a lot of the non-League clubs has disappeared. That is one reason why Hull City have been able to escape possible embarrassment on so many occasions, but even when they have been in the bottom two divisions and had to join the fray in the first round proper, they have not succumbed. A gap of 90 years between the defeats against Tottenham and Hednesford is a record that many League clubs, particularly some of soccer's traditionally lesser lights, would envy.

At the same time the Tigers have been given a few stern reminders that they should always guard against complacency on such occasions and it is curious that three of their biggest frights have come against opposition from the North-East, an area accepted as one of England's noted hotbeds of soccer. Such instances have led to some great matches in the acknowledged FA Cup tradition – at least for any neutral observers – and huge collective sighs of relief from City and their followers when the drama abated and reputations remained intact.

But the first time that the Tigers had a close shave against non-League opposition came relatively soon after the defeat against Spurs in 1907 and it happened against another side who have long since established themselves as FA Premiership regulars, Southampton. In 1914-15 City had beaten First Division West Bromwich Albion 1-0 in the first round and then defeated non-League Northampton Town 2-1, also at home. That earned them a trip to Southern League side Southampton at the Dell on February 20, 1915, and the Tigers toned up for the tie at Worthing.

And on the Wednesday before the game the City party witnessed a drama that was to end in tragedy. The Worthing lifeboat was launched in a rainstorm to go to the aid of a schooner-rigged vessel and twice capsized in heavy seas. The crew were thrown into the water, but clung on to the sides and managed to get on board again with the exception of one of their number, Jack Burgess, who was washed away and died soon after being pulled ashore at Goring. Southampton, meanwhile, was described as "nothing more nor less than a huge military camp or centre" in those dark times and, as regards the match itself, City made two changes after William "Tim" Wright had been passed fit with Doug Morgan and Billy Halligan returning in place of John Pattison and Henry Turner.

The tie itself had plenty of excitement for the 15,607 crowd with City going ahead when Jack Lee set up a goal for William "Kilty" Cameron, but Len Andrews dramatically equalised for the Saints three minutes from the end. The Tigers then played extra time, which had just been introduced, for the first time in their history and in the first period then went behind for the first time in the match when Fred Jones made it 2-1 to Southampton. City were struggling because of injuries to "Tim" Wright and Charles Betts and luck had certainly not been on Halligan's side because he had had two efforts disallowed and hit the post twice at various points. But in the 116th minute the Tigers survived with a 2-2 draw when the dangerous David Mercer centred and Lee popped up with the equaliser. Both sides went close to a winner in a frantic finale, but a replay was necessary at Anlaby Road a week later.

This time an 11,000 crowd saw the Tigers make no mistake after being just four minutes from losing to a non-League side. Cameron and Lee were again on target, but Sammy Stevens, who was denied three possible penalties over the two games, scored twice as Southampton were savaged 4-0. That earned City a place in the fourth round for the first time when they controversially lost 4-2 at First Division Bolton Wanderers – a game that was curiously to be remembered for the penalties that were given rather than those that were turned down.

The Tigers' first great FA Cup nail-biter against the non-League hordes from the North-East came in the 1962-63 season when they were drawn at home to Crook Town in the first round. In the previous two seasons City had comfortably accounted for non-League sides Sutton Town and Rhyl respectively at the first-round stage, but they were given the shock of their lives on November 3, 1962.

There was an ominous ring to City's pre-match preparations. Wing-half Eric McMillan damaged a knee in training, but came through a fitness check satisfactorily. Then another wing-half, Les Collinson, dropped a concrete block on his foot in an accident at home and was ruled out of the tie. In the meantime, Len Sharpe, who was already developing a reputation as a utility man in his first season with the club, recovered well from a thigh injury that he had received against Queen's Park Rangers in a League game and was earmarked as Collinson's replacement. But then

Ray Henderson, who scored Hull City's first and last goals in their 5-4 win over Crook Town in the FA Cup at Boothferry Park in November 1962.

he suffered a clash of heads with Brian Garvey in training and needed three stitches in an eye wound. Eventually he played with the stitches in.

Northern League Crook, though, were without two of their England amateur internationals who had helped them to win the FA Amateur Cup in 1961-62. Centre-forward Arnold Coates was a long-term casualty with knee trouble, while teenager Frank Clark, later better-known as the manager of Leyton Orient, Nottingham Forest and Manchester City, signed part-time professional forms for Newcastle United during the build-up to the tie at Boothferry Park. And Clark's replacement at left-back, 17-year-old Roy Gale, was available to play only after he had been given permission to miss a school match on the same day. But Town could boast three other England amateur internationals – Derek Gardener, Jimmy

John McSeveney, who scored twice for Hull City when they beat Crook Town 5-4 in the FA Cup at Boothferry Park in November 1962.

McMillan and Peter Garbutt, who later joined Carlisle United – and another 17-year-old, John Cocking, whom ex-Tiger Don Revie, then Leeds United's manager, came to watch in the cup tie.

There was not too much for the Tigers to worry about in the early stages because Ray Henderson gave them the lead after just 11 minutes, but then they were stunned by a three-goal burst by Crook. After 28 minutes their centre-forward Ken Bowron, who later played League soccer for Workington, equalised with a shot from the edge of the penalty area. But then Cocking and Garbutt scored with long-range drives in the 36th and 37th minutes respectively and City went into halftime 3-1 down. If the interval gave City time to regroup and try to regain some composure, then matters took a turn for the even worse four minutes into the second half when Cocking headed home a cross by Don Sparks to give Town a 4-1 advantage.

Hull City's Doug Clarke takes on Crook Town's Alan Brown in the FA Cup tie at Boothferry Park in November 1962.

Crook Town's Alan Brown (left) watches as his young colleague Roy Gale heads clear under pressure from Hull City's Chris Chilton in the FA Cup at Boothferry Park in November 1962.

Fortunately for the Tigers, they pulled back one goal only two minutes later when John McSeveney pounced on an error by Crook's captain Barry Storey. It gave them hope, but it was still 4-2 with only 20 minutes remaining and it was only then that City produced an amazing comeback that would have done justice to Frank Sinatra in another sphere. They concocted their own three-goal cocktail in a nine-minute spell as the darkness began to set in and it was good enough to win them the match 5-4. Chris Chilton nodded in a centre from Dudley Price to make it 4-3 and a minute later McSeveney equalised after Doug Clarke has carved out the opening. Henderson had scored 11 minutes after the start, so he aptly added his second 11 minutes before the end. The Tigers scraped through and sportingly applauded their Crook rivals from the field as most of the 9,484 crowd breathed a collective sigh of relief.

McSeveney, who has latterly scouted for Derby County and Ipswich Town, recalls the excitement of it all and analyses the tie as a classic of a certain type. He said:"I can remember all the goals that day. Chris Chilton's was a cracker, but I can remember Ray Henderson's winner because I was standing right behind him at the time. It was a header. And I've often quoted the Crook match as an example of what can happen if you get too cocky and confident. Crook got that way and I remember making it 4-2 after someone had tried to be too clever with a backpass and I nipped in. But they also began to get very tired as we fought back."

Henderson, City's other two-goal marksman, cannot recall his winner: instead he remembers more of manager Cliff Britton's halftime pep talk to his players when they went in 3-1 in arrears. He said:"Cliff seemed to have this great fetish for the FA Cup, probably because he got wound up like everyone else with every game being like life and death. And to have lost to an amateur side would have been the end of the world for him. I think that a certain amount of panic had crept in by halftime. Cliff was ashen-faced and I've always said that I would have given a fiver to have seen his face when we went 4-1 down almost immediately after we'd kicked off for the second half. But once we realised that Crook were running out of steam, there was nothing in it and we could have had six or seven goals by the finish. They suddenly caved in after our second goal and then we had a header disallowed, which incensed us a bit. We felt then that we'd have them struggling once we got through them. But although I can remember my first goal, which was from a through ball that broke to me on the edge of the penalty box, I honestly can't recall the winner."

It is just as well that McSeveney can remember the goal that saw the Tigers through and it is just as well that it happened to spare their blushes. In the second round McSeveney himself again scored twice as City beat Workington 2-0 at Boothferry Park, but that was the end of the club's FA Cup success that season. As a particularly harsh winter dragged on, the Tigers lost 2-0 at home to Leyton Orient after extra time after Chilton had scored for them in a 1-1 draw at Brisbane Road.

As 1980 wore on, City were struggling to avoid the drop into the old Fourth Division for the first time. And the last thing that any League side need when their general form has deserted them is a cup tie against potential upstarts from a lower grade. All of a sudden it may be open to question as to who really are supposed to be the underdogs. There were few scares in the first round of the FA Cup as the Tigers defeated Fourth Division Halifax Town 2-1 with two goals by Keith Edwards at Boothferry Park. But then they faced a second-round tie at home to Northern League side Blyth Spartans, whose giantkilling exploits had incredibly taken them to the fifth round of the competition three seasons earlier, on December 13.

To intensify the situation, City were also facing two players with a point to prove to them. Blyth's goalkeeper Dave Clarke had had a trial with the Tigers as a 14-year-old, but he had damaged his wrist in a training accident involving Ken Wagstaff and had been unable to do himself justice. Instead he had become an England non-League international, as had one of his teammates, striker Les Mutrie, who passed a fitness test on the morning of the match. In addition, Blyth's midfield player Paul Walker had had a brief spell with the Tigers when he was a regular in their reserves before trying his luck with Doncaster Rovers.

The Tigers were without their ineligible recent signings Steve Hoolickin and Billy Whitehurst, so Bobby McNeil came in at right-back and Craig Norrie played up front after recovering from an ankle injury. Micky Horswill was sidelined by an Achilles tendon injury, but City had problems at centre-back, where John Roberts was ruled out because of knee trouble and Dale Roberts was missing after damaging a knee in training. But Steve Richards was recalled and Stuart Croft passed a fitness test on a calf problem.

Everything went well for City in the early stages even though Spartans adopted a physical approach at times and Keith Edwards gave them the lead after just nine minutes. Blyth's spirit enabled them to fight back, though, and twice they hit the woodwork through Alan Barker and Tony Boylan. The Tigers, in turn, hit the bar with a header by Croft and a fierce drive from Nick Deacy, but they could not add to their lead and ten minutes from the end Blyth stunned the 6,050 crowd. David Mitchinson headed down Walker's centre, Mutrie swept home their equaliser and it ended 1-1.

The ensuing draw offered the winners a home game against Fourth Division Doncaster Rovers in the third round, but the Tigers, who had signed Brian Ferguson from Newcastle United on trial in the interim after new manager Arthur Cox had freed him, could hardly relish a trip to Croft Park for the replay because they had not won an away game since September 1979. They named the same starting line-up after Croft had come through a further check on his nagging calf problem, but Blyth were forced to make one change, Ray Young replacing Boylan, who had been carried off on a stretcher with damaged ankle ligaments 19 minutes before the end of the first meeting. Spartans' manager Jackie Marks remained reserved about his side's chances in the replay three days later, but his coach Gary Moore tried to increase the pressure on City by saying: "We must fancy our chances. We were the better side at Hull and deserved to win."

Stuart Croft, whose goal saw Hull City safely through against Blyth Spartans in their FA Cup replay at Elland Road, Leeds, in December 1980.

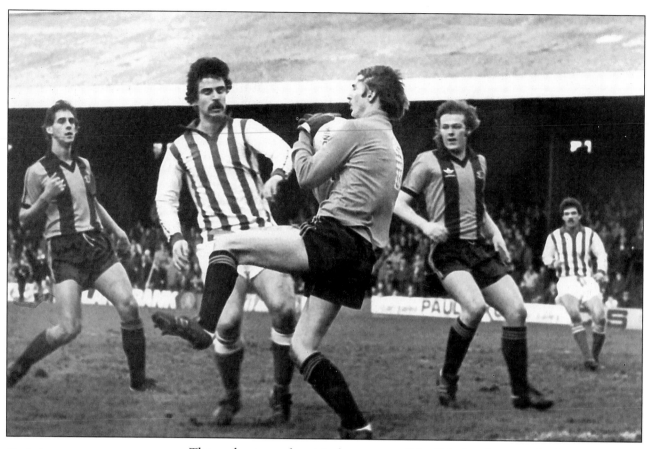

Hull City's goal-keeper Tony Norman beats Blyth Spartans' Les Mutrie, who was later to be his team-mate, to the ball during the FA Cup at Boothferry Park in December 1980. City defenders Steve Richards (left) and Stuart Croft watch.

The replay turned out to be an eventful affair for the crowd of 6,050 as both sides sought to gain the upper hand. Blyth went ahead through Mutrie after 17 minutes when he was set up by Gerry Hogan and Terry Johnson and his 20-yard drive flew in off the woodwork. But the Tigers drew level after 39 minutes when Norrie scored his first goal of the season with a header that went through Clarke's hands after Croft had nodded down Brian Marwood's corner. But two minutes later Spartans were back in front when Mutrie provided the opportunity for Young to score with a shot that went in off the underside of the bar. Young hit the bar soon

Hull City's Steve Richards tackles Blyth Spartans' Gerry Hogan during the FA Cup tie at Boothferry Park in December 1980. City's Gordon Nisbet provides extra defensive cover.

afterwards and in the second half Steve Richards and Croft hit the woodwork for the Tigers, but time was beginning to run out for them. And it was not until six minutes from the end that Edwards threw them a lifeline with his 11th goal of what was a generally-barren season for the club all-round. He outpaced Tommy Dixon as he ran on to a through ball from his close friend Garreth Roberts and took the tie into extra time.

There was still time for some more drama and it happened in the 102nd minute when Blyth were awarded a penalty after Richards was ruled to have handled in a scramble as Mutrie tried to force the ball home for the winner. It might be unfair to ask City goalkeeper Tony Norman to estimate the importance of his wedding on the day before the match in comparison with heroics on the night after it! But he rescued the Tigers, initially by guessing right when Mutrie side-footed his spot-kick to his left and then by blocking substitute Paul Ross's fierce follow-up. It ended 2-2 and City survived again as the action switched to Leeds United's Elland Road ground for the second replay on December 22.

City lost a League game 3-1 at Sheffield United in-between and manager Mike Smith was left with a poser at right-back because he had agreed to sell the dependable Gordon Nisbet to Plymouth Argyle for £30,000 to the consternation of a lot of fans. With Hoolickin unavailable, Smith plumped for Dennis Booth, whom he had signed as a midfield player, to fill the vacancy, while defender John Roberts returned to the side after injury to the exclusion of Richards. Blyth retained the same starting line-up, while British Rail ran an FA Cup special train for City fans to a game for the first time since 1973.

The crowd of 5,914 watched a goalless first half, but the Tigers went in front after 64 minutes when Norrie exchanged passes with Steve McClaren and scored from 20 yards when Clarke could not hang on to his shot. But five minutes from time there was to be another penalty drama when Spartans were handed an escape route after Bobby McNeil had tussled with Johnson. It looked as if a free-kick should have been awarded outside the penalty box for the first challenge, but the second clash brought a spot-kick. Mutrie shot wide from it, but Tony Norman was adjudged to have moved too soon and it had to be retaken. This time Mutrie made no mistake. It was extra time again with the score 1-1.

Hogan had an effort disallowed before the Tigers finally sealed victory with six minutes of the extra period left. They won a corner, McClaren swung it over and Croft headed it home for his first goal for nearly 14 months. It finished 2-1 and the plans for a third replay at Middlesbrough's Ayresome Park headquarters were quickly forgotten.

The Tigers then beat Doncaster Rovers 1-0 at home in the third round with a goal by Deacy, but they went out at the next hurdle although a crowd of 37,432 saw them put up a determined display before losing 2-0 to Tottenham Hotspur at White Hart Lane. There was, however, another intriguing post-script to that second replay against Blyth at Leeds because immediately after the match City became involved in negotiations to sign Les Mutrie. The fee of £30,000 was excessive for a non-League player, but it gave Mutrie the chance to atone for the disappointments that he had had when he had last tried to break into League soccer on a regular basis with Carlisle United. This time he was to make the most of it.

In the 1996-97 season the Tigers were again drawn against Northern League opposition in the FA Cup. Again they could not beat them at the first time of asking, again they became embroiled in an extra-time drama and again they finally got through by the skin of their teeth. This time their opponents were Whitby Town, whose side included Lawrie Pearson, who had helped the Tigers to promotion from the old Third Division in 1984-85 and had become Middlesbrough's Football in the Community officer. In addition, City, by then in the Third Division, had been drawn away, but the tie was switched to Scarborough on a wet Sunday and it attracted a gate of only 3,337 on November 17, 1996. The Tigers called up Jamie Marks at right-back for his first game of the season because of injuries to Simon Trevitt and Kenny Gilbert, while Mark Greaves replaced the suspended Rob Dewhurst as they prepared to face an experienced Whitby side managed by Harry Dunn, who had been a Wembley winner with Scarborough in the FA Trophy.

The torrential rain that left surface water on the pitch was the only winner on this occasion and the game finished as a goalless draw with City manager Terry Dolan summing it up as "a good, old-fashioned cup tie." Both sides missed some clear-cut chances, but the most significant moment came after 22 minutes when the Tigers lost striker Duane Darby with damaged knee ligaments. Darby was unhappy to be substituted and stormed straight down the players' tunnel from the pitch, but Dolan responded by insisting: "Sometimes we have got to play with our heads rather than our hearts and although he might not have liked it, I have more experience than he has."

Whitby kept the same starting line-up for the replay at Boothferry Park nine days later after defenders Alan Martin and David Logan had passed fitness tests, but City were forced to ring the changes. They had incurred three injury problems in a goalless draw in an intervening League game at Exeter City, so goalkeeper Roy Carroll was missing with a shoulder injury, Gregor Rioch was out because of a damaged hamstring and Greaves was sidelined as a result of a bruised foot. Steve Wilson took over in goal, Scott Maxfield replaced Rioch and Dewhurst had completed his suspension.

Darby had patched up his difference of opinion with City's management and he was to play a record-breaking role in what was to become the highest-scoring competitive game at Boothferry Park with an aggregate of 12 goals. The Tigers had beaten Carlisle United 11-1 at Anlaby Road in a Third Division North game in 1939 and there had also been a 10-3 home over the Coldstream Guards – curiously on April 1, 1905 – in the days before they became a Football League club. But this cup tie, watched by only 2,900 fans because of their general discontent with the way in which the Tigers were being run at the time, was to have numerous twists and turns before its outcome became clear and it became a personal triumph for Darby.

After eight minutes he opened the scoring from Andy Brown's long ball, but Whitby's prolific marksman Paul Pitman, who had been sent off in an FA Vase tie between the FA Cup clashes, equalised a minute later. And in the 20th minute Town went ahead when Graham Robinson scored from John Borthwick's pass as the Tigers' claims that he had been offside were dismissed. But Darby then tipped the scales City's way to complete a first-half hat-trick, following up to score after half-an-hour when Whitby goalkeeper David Campbell failed to hold Marks' shot and

Duane Darby, Hull City's six-goal hero against Whitby Town in the FA Cup in November 1996.

then adding a third from Richard Peacock's pass a minute before half-time. But Pitman incredibly completed his own hat-trick with two penalties in quick succession to put Whitby 4-3 ahead. The first came in the 47th minute when Wilson fouled Robinson and the second was awarded two minutes later when Dewhurst handled a centre by Logan. The Tigers were within a whisker of an embarrassing cup exit, but Darby rescued them with his fourth goal in the final minute of normal time when he made it 4-4 from Ian Wright's cross.

City steeled themselves for extra time and they finally took control of the dicey situation. After 92 minutes Peacock put them back in front at long last from Scott Maxfield's cross and almost at once Darby pounced on a mistake for his fifth goal to make it 6-4. He then added his record-breaking sixth goal after 107 minutes when he backheeled the ball home from Neil Mann's cross before Mann himself made it 8-4 when he scored from inside the penalty area with three minutes left.

Duane Darby had set a club record by scoring six times in an accepted first-team competitive match, beating the five recorded by Ken McDonald and Simon Raleigh in League games in 1928 and 1930 respectively. What made his feat all the more exceptional was the fact that he had been doubtful for the cup tie because of a sore knee and a touch of influenza. He said:"At halftime I saw the doctor because I was having trouble breathing, but I decided to play on. I never thought we were going out and we just kept plugging away. I always thought we might do it, but I never thought that I would ever get six goals in a game. It is something that you can only dream about." That night his dream came true as he wrote himself into City folklore.

But one way or another, it was a further dramatic case of what might have been. As against Crook Town, the Tigers had conceded four goals at home in the FA Cup to a non-League side at Boothferry Park and still survived to fight another day. On this occasion they lost 5-1 at home to Crewe Alexandra, who were to win promotion to the First Division via the Play-offs at the end of the season, in the second round. But before that, another chapter in their book of great escapes had been written.

Chapter Seven

Up, Up and Away

IT IS not just a well-worn cliche to describe Hull City's loyal fans as long-suffering. They quite simply have been – too often for too long. If you gauge a club's historical League standing by the number of seasons that they have either spent in the top flight or won promotion, then there is not much in the shape of solace for followers of the Tigers. The facts of their soccer life insist that not only have they never been among England's club elite, but on only six occasions have their achieved promotion. Of those six, only three campaigns have brought championships. It does not add up to much on a club's soccer curriculum vitae or suggest an overflowing trophy cabinet when placed in the context of almost a century of trying.

Yet it is a touch ironic that during some of their promotion seasons, City have undoubtedly shown what potential they have if only their powers-that-be had been able to get things right on a consistent basis. They scored goals with a greedy readiness in their first four promotion seasons: in the latter two in the 1980s the club were again thinking and starting to act big under ebullient chairman Don Robinson. They were always to fall short of reaching the top flight, but they gave their fans some special exciting moments on the way there. They had a penchant for going up in some style on the few occasions that they achieved it.

City fans had to wait until the 1932-33 season to enjoy promotion for the first time, but it was well worth the wait for a lot of reasons. The Tigers went up as the champions of the Third Division North, pipping Wrexham by two points and Stockport County by a further three. They scored 100 League goals from 42 games in a season, Bill McNaughton setting up an all-time club record with 41 of them in 41 appearances. Russell Wainscoat accounted for a further 21 goals in 34 League games, while full-back Cliff Woodhead had the only ever-present record in terms of appearances. Their record at Anlaby Road was nigh impeccable because they were undefeated at home in a season for the only time in their history. They won 18 and drew three of their 21 League games at home and scored a club-record total of 69 goals in them. City also conceded just 45 goals and that gave them the second-best defensive record in the country that season behind Second Division champions Stoke City.

The manager Haydn Green, who had played for Nottingham Forest, Manchester United, Aston Villa and Reading, replaced Bill McCracken, who had resigned at the end of the 1930-31 season, and relied heavily on experience as he tried to rebuild the playing side. In November 1931, for example, he acquired the services of former England centre-half Jack Hill from Bradford City: he was to captain the promotion side of 1932-33 and also succeed Green as manager. Green also converted Bert "Paddy" Mills to wing-half and signed wingers Fred Forward, who played for the club in just that one promotion season, from Portsmouth and Charlie Sargeant from Bristol City, introduced wing-half Stanley Denby, a recruit from Goole Town, and snapped up wing-half Tommy Gardner from Grimsby Town.

The side gelled remarkably quickly although McNaughton, a Londoner from Poplar, proved to be Green's most inspired signing during the summer of 1932 when he moved to Anlaby Road from Gateshead. Wainscoat was the more prolific marksman in the early stages of the promotion season because McNaughton did not score in his first three League games for the club: that, though, was amazingly his longest sequence without a League goal during that campaign. He then scored in three successive games before signalling his intent in imposing fashion with a hat-trick in a 4-0 home win over Southport and four goals in a 5-1 victory over Barnsley at Anlaby Road a week later. McNaughton was to record only one other hat-trick that season – in a 4-1 home success over Mansfield Town – but he gave little respite to Third Division North defences because he scored two goals in a League game on eight other occasions.

Wainscoat, who had made one England appearance in 1929, had already had one productive season with the Tigers before helping them to promotion, but he registered a hat-trick of his own in a 5-0 home win over New Brighton and ticked over nicely with the goals apart from during a mid-season spell when he missed a number of matches. Even then there was support at that time from Scottish inside-forward Andrew Duncan, who hit a hat-trick in a 6-1 triumph over Doncaster Rovers at Anlaby Road.

Although the Tigers won only one of their opening four League games, two of which were against their close rivals Wrexham, they then won five of their next six and soon afterwards embarked on a run from late October to the end of January in which they were undefeated in 13 League outings. They did not draw a League game in the second half of the season from the advent of 1933 and gradually they moved inexorably towards promotion. The best League crowd of the season – 20,248 – saw City crucially beat Chester 2-0 at home on April 1 and a fortnight later they registered their second 6-1 win of the season at Anlaby Road when they trounced Carlisle United. It should be remembered that only the champions earned promotion in the Third Division North format, but at that stage the Tigers returned to the top of the table on goal average over Chester, who were then their main rivals.

Two days later City completed their Easter programme when they gained swift revenge over Tranmere Rovers, who had beaten them 2-0 at home on Good Friday. The Tigers won the return game at Anlaby Road 3-0 with McNaughton opening the scoring from the penalty spot before he and Wainscoat helped to set up further goals for each other. It was three wins in a row when the Tigers came from behind to win 2-1 at struggling York City and they led the table by three points at that stage from Wrexham, who had a game in hand. But both Wrexham and Chester, who had finished their home programme, still had to go to fourth-placed Stockport County, so City just had to keep their nerve and they did do with a 3-0 win over Crewe Alexandra at Anlaby Road in which skipper Hill scored his only League goal of the campaign before being forced to play on the wing after receiving a black eye and a swollen jaw in one clash.

And on May 1, 1933, City achieved promotion for the first time in their history when they beat York City 2-1 at home to complete a quick double over them. Stockport extended their unbeaten run to 15 games with a 1-0 success at home to Wrexham to leave them four points behind the Tigers with only one fixture left. Fittingly, McNaughton scored City's two goals, the first of which was another penalty, against York in the opening 47 minutes, while goalkeeper George "Geordie" Maddison demonstrated his bravery by playing on despite tearing ligaments in his left shoulder after only ten minutes.

The scenes of celebration were unyielding and it was reported: "After the game pent-up excitement was released, the playing pitch was invaded and some of the players were joyfully mobbed before they could complete a hasty retreat to the dressing-room. Some of the spectators demonstrated their jubilation by throwing high the cushions which are hired by grandstand occupants. This gleeful gesture developed into a veritable cushion battle and for some time the air was black with hundreds of whizzing cushions. The ceasefire was sounded when members of the team, accompanied by directors of the club, made their appearance in the front of the stand to receive the cheers of the thousands of supporters."

After the match City's directors, officials and players attended a dinner and dance at Field's restaurant in the city's King Edward Street, while congratulatory messages soon arrived from Hull FC, Hull Kingston Rovers, Hull and East Riding, Arsenal, Tottenham Hotspur, Grimsby Town, Lincoln City and Stoke City. And John Bielby, who was in his first year as City's president, said: "It is particularly gratifying to find the Tigers certain of getting back again into the company to which we were bold enough to apply for admission in the second year of the club's history. I think it can certainly be said that the players have reaped the reward of consistency this season. Their success is the outcome of really good teamwork and team spirit, allied to the all-round ability to play football of a superior quality to that of the majority of their rivals."

City Supporters' Club, meanwhile, issued the following public plea: "We are very anxious to recover fully 100 cushions which disappeared from City's ground in the general jubilation at the end of the match with York. It is feared that many of the cushions were taken away as souvenirs of a happy event, but if those responsible realise that it will mean a loss of fully £10 to replace them and to repair others that were damaged and that this amount of money represents our whole season's efforts on behalf of the football club, it is believed that they will return the missing articles to the groundsman at Anlaby Road…"

It was a classic piece of City anti-climax, of course, and it was matched by defeat in the last game of the season at lowly Rochdale. The Tigers, who were without the injured Maddison and Wainscoat because of a bereavement, needed two goals to take their League tally to 100 in a season for the first time. They got them thanks to the redoubtable McNaughton, who scored twice in two minutes, but they lost 3-2 with Rochdale's winner coming from a penalty as England amateur international goalkeeper Edgar Ainsworth made an unhappy debut for City because he, too, picked up an injury. "Paddy" Mills' second spell with the club ended when he was not retained and the same fate befell full-back Arthur Rodgers, but it was otherwise joy all-round.

An even more joyful era awaited City when former England international Raich Carter agreed to join the club from Derby County as player-coach. The only person who was presumably somewhat less gleeful about the prospect was the manager,

Hull City chairman Harold Needler (left) with Raich Carter, who masterminded the 1948-49 promotion season.

Major Frank Buckley, who resigned soon afterwards. It automatically paved the way for "the silver-haired genius" to become player-manager instead of Buckley's assistant.

Carter had been hoping to break into management and City had to fend off competition from Notts County, who wanted him only as a player, and Nottingham Forest for his services. The news of the Tigers' interest became public knowledge towards the end of March 1948 and a seven-strong delegation of directors confronted Carter in Derby's boardroom. He moved to the Tigers in a £6,000 deal and made his debut at home to York City on April 3. Nine days later Buckley took charge at Leeds United and on April 23 it was confirmed that Carter would be City's new player-manager with effect from the end of the season.

Carter said:"I shall do my best to justify the confidence which the City board have placed in me. My aim will be to foster the game and improve the standard of football. You cannot command success on the field – you must strive to attain it." He soon did away with the constant chopping and changing that had been a feature of Buckley's approach. He used just 12 players in the opening nine games of the 1948-49 season – Andy Conway replacing Willie Buchan at inside-left on three occasions – and the Tigers won them all to create a new Football League record.

The ninth victory to smash a 45-year-old record was a 2-1 triumph at Accrington Stanley and on the way back City stopped off for a meal at an Ilkley hotel, where they were congratulated by the Australian rugby-league squad. The team coach was then met by police cars and motorcycle outriders from the outskirts of Hull and it was escorted to a civic reception at the floodlit Regal Cinema in the heart of the city. An estimated 12,000 crowd had congregated in Ferensway and Carter told them: "Tonight you are welcoming back a team who have played good football. I can honestly say that I have been very proud and pleased to come to Hull City. We have a long way to go to the end of the season and the task ahead is very hard, but I hope to see a bigger crowd round this theatre in May because I trust that we can win a place in the Second Division." Trainer George Lax then led the players in singing Carter's theme song: "When Your Hair Has Turned To Silver."

When Jack Taylor, Allan Mellor and George King came in for their first appearances of the season in the 10th game instead of Norman Fowler, Denis Durham and Norman Moore, City's winning run ended: they managed only a goalless draw at Doncaster Rovers even though the gate of 37,149 was to be the biggest in their League history. And the crowds at Boothferry Park were exceptional, rarely dropping below the 30,000 mark and the opposition included clubs such as New Brighton, Accrington Stanley, Barrow, Doncaster Rovers and Southport as well as current League clubs such as Rochdale, Hartlepool United, Darlington and Chester, who have never been renowned for playing in front of large attendances on a regular basis. When Rotherham United, who posed the only serious threat to the Tigers' promotion challenge, came to Boothferry Park on Christmas Day 1948, a crowd of 49,655 packed the ground.

In 1948-49 the Tigers may not have had the kind of goalscoring partnership who were to distinguish most of their other promotion campaigns, but it did not detract from their capacity to be on the mark regularly. They scored 93 goals in 42 League games and only mid-table Third Division South side Notts County did better with 102. City put six goals past Oldham Athletic, Halifax Town and

Stockport County: Southport and Crewe Alexandra got off a little more lightly by conceding only five. Norman Moore was the top goalscorer with 22 goals in 31 League games: he was born in Grimsby and he joined City from Grimsby Town, for whom three close members of his family played, but he knew where his loyalties were because he once told me: "I'm a Grimsby lad, but I've no real love for Town. I'm a proper Hull supporter, I enjoyed my times with them, the people were marvellous and the crowd were always very good to me. Besides, they gave me more money with Hull in the Third Division than I'd been getting with Grimsby in the First!"

Moore was well-supported in the goalscoring stakes by Carter himself, Ken Harrison and Danish international Viggo Jensen, who was signed as an amateur from EFB Esbjerg towards the end of October 1948. He scored on his debut in a 4-1 home win over New Brighton and immediately impressed his new teammates because wing-half Jimmy Greenhalgh later said:"Viggo Jensen opened the door to skills we'd never heard of and I have abiding memories of the range of his ability. For example, he was the first player to pull a ball down on his instep. We hadn't seen that kind of technical ability before." Greenhalgh modestly saw his own contribution in a different light because he added: "I was a working-class player who would never be classed as a great player. But I was a reasonably good professional and the only kickback I get from my playing days is a feeling of satisfaction."

Greenhalgh and centre-half Harold Meens missed only three games between them in that promotion campaign and were the only survivors in that team of the City line-up for the first-ever game at Boothferry Park against Lincoln City at the end of August 1946. And defensively, City were simply the best. They conceded just

Jimmy Greenhalgh (left), who played in the first game at Boothferry Park and also helped Hull City to promotion in 1948-49.

Harold Meens (right), Hull City's stalwart centre-half during their 1948-49 promotion campaign.

28 goals – the best record of all the 88 League clubs in 1948-49. They conceded four at Bradford City, three at home to York City and two against Halifax Town, Rotherham United and Chester in games that they still won. The other 15 League goals were parsimoniously given away in ones. Meens later recalled: "Our defensive record was one of the best City ever had and I was really proud to be a member of that particular side. As a manager, Raich promoted team spirit, he involved the players and their wives in everything and it was as if the club were a family concern. We used to play for one another and if one player was having an off-day, then we would do our best to keep the ball away from him."

And it all added up to just four League defeats – at home to Darlington, away to Bradford City, at home to York City and at home to Doncaster Rovers. That one away defeat in a season was naturally a club record. In-between the Tigers went on

Norman Moore, Hull City's leading goalscorer during the 1948-49 promotion season.

unbeaten runs of 11, 12, seven and seven matches. It was no wonder that it was such a golden era for the club.

Winger Ken Harrison was the only ever-present, but there was stability and even those players who were on the fringes of it all played their parts. Take centre-forward Bill Price, for example. He was signed from Reading in January 1949, scored a respectable five times in just eight League appearances as Norman Moore's deputy in that promotion season, never played in the first team again and was allowed to move on to Bradford City before the year out. He once told me: "I enjoyed it at Hull and the 1948-49 season wasn't bad at all for the club. I thought I did all right because I scored twice in my first match. We had a few decent players and a good team when Raich signed me and I was surprised when he told me that he was willing to give me a transfer. I wished I'd stayed with them longer, but I think that the main trouble was that Norman Moore was more popular than I was!"

Promotion became increasingly inevitable even though Rotherham United kept within striking distance of the Tigers. It was effectively confirmed after the 6-1 hiding handed out to Stockport County at Boothferry Park on April 30, 1949, when the Millers could only draw 1-1 with Carlisle United. Rotherham's goal average was considerably inferior to that of City and the fans were convinced that, barring a soccer miracle, their dreams had come true. At the end of the game against Stockport, they chanted for Carter and, wearing a mackintosh over his shirt and a towel round his neck, he duly addressed them from the stands after they had vaulted over fences, surged on to the pitch and surrounded the entrance to the dressing-rooms.

Hull City celebrate promotion in 1948-49 with an end-of-season dinner at the city's Royal Station Hotel.

Bob Brocklebank, Hull City's manager during the 1958-59 promotion season.

Two days later City contrived to lose 1-0 to Doncaster Rovers in their final home game of the season, but Carter and popular goalkeeper Billy Bly addressed the fans afterwards before everyone went off to Hull's Royal Station Hotel for a celebratory dinner, which was followed by a film show at the Regal Cinema. The Tigers needed to lose 10-0 at Carlisle in their final match of the season and Rotherham, whose long-serving manager Reg Freeman had long since telephoned his congratulations to Carter, needed to beat Gateshead 19-0. Not surprisingly, neither happened. City, who were without Carter because of ankle injury, drew 1-1 at Carlisle and finished a memorable season three points clear of Rotherham.

There was a new look to the Football League structure for the 1958-59 season and the Tigers were to make the most of it. A year earlier it had been agreed that the old Third Division North and Third Division South would be replaced by the new, de-regionalised Third Division and Fourth Division. Accordingly, the top non-promoted 11 sides of each section would form 22 members of the new Third Division and were to be augmented by the relegated duo from the Second Division, Doncaster Rovers and Notts County in this instance. Since their own relegation in 1955-56 City had comfortably held down a place in the top half of the Third Division North in the following two seasons, finishing eighth and fifth respectively. Manager Bob Brocklebank had introduced a number of younger players – they were known as the Brocklebank Toddlers at one point to rival Manchester United's Busby Babes – but he had an experienced squad at his disposal when the Tigers took their place in the new Third Division.

Two club stalwarts, goalkeeper Billy Bly and left-half or left-back Denis Durham, had played in the promotion side of 1948-49 season under Raich Carter's management, but things did not initially augur well under the new structure in 1958-59 season. City won only one of their opening seven games and scored just

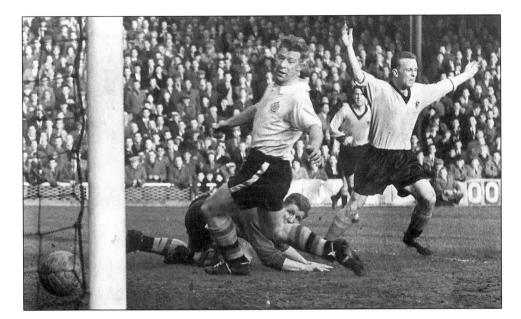

Bill Bradbury forces the ball past Stockport County's goalkeeper Arthur Barnard and defender Gordon Wilmott in Hull City's 3-1 home win in February 1959.

Bill Bradbury beats defender James Lawlor to score the second goal of his hat-trick in Hull City's 4-0 home win over Bradford City at Boothferry Park in January 1959.

five goals in them. In the final match of the sequence they were hammered 6-1 at Southampton and a long, hard winter was looking likely because Bill Bradbury, Brian Bulless and Brian Cripsey had all sought transfers.

But the debacle at the Dell proved to be a watershed in City's fortunes that season because they then won four games in succession and the goals began to flow. They were helped by three successive home games in a week, but they beat Notts County 5-0, Accrington Stanley 4-2 and Brentford 3-1. Another ordinary run was then followed by six wins in succession up to the start of December. City had gone out of the FA Cup with a woeful first-round display at home to Stockport County, to whom they lost 1-0, but they were becoming single-minded in the League. By the end of the year they put five more goals past Bournemouth, Doncaster Rovers and Mansfield Town. The scoring sprees included hat-tricks by Bradbury and Colin Smith, who were becoming a lethal twin spearhead.

Bradbury claimed another hat-trick in a 4-0 home win over Bradford City in early January 1959 and the month ended with revenge over Southampton at Boothferry Park. That 3-0 success sparked a run of six consecutive wins that brought

Hull City's top scorer Bill Bradbury is escorted past adoring fans after he had helped the team to achieve promotion against Bury at Boothferry Park in April 1959.

a tally of 17 goals. Above all, the Tigers' home form was near impeccable. They had drawn their first two home games against Plymouth Argyle and Swindon Town during the moderate start, they lost 3-2 to Newport County in early October and they drew 3-3 with shock FA Cup semi-finalists Norwich City in an Easter clash that attracted the biggest crowd of the season, 24,156. Quite simply, they won the rest of their League games at Boothferry Park – 19 out of 23.

Promotion was clinched with a 2-0 home win over Bury in the penultimate game of the season when close friends Bill Bradbury and Brian Bulless were on the

Brian Bulless scores one of the goals that sealed promotion for Hull City in 1958-59 in a 2-0 home win over Bury in April 1959.

mark, but City wrapped up the season on a low when they then lost 5-1 at Wrexham. Bradbury's goal against Bury had enabled him to set a club postwar record of 30 League goals in a season. He had played in 45 games and his partner Smith scored 26 goals in 40 League appearances. Doug Clarke chipped in with 12 goals and David Coates with nine as the Tigers finished as runners-up, one point behind Plymouth Argyle, who finished on 62. A draw in that final game at Wrexham, though, would have given City the title.

There had been moments when it was a topsy-turvy season with the early-season transfer requests and the thrashing at Southampton in addition to the over-all success of it all. In addition, manager Bob Brocklebank became a target for Leeds United towards the end of March 1959 even though he still had two years of his contract with City remaining: he was rewarded instead with a five-year extension to his deal at Boothferry Park.

Hull City's players and officials celebrate promotion in the dressing-room after the win over Bury at Boothferry Park in April 1959.

David Coates beats Reading defender Eddie McLaren and goalkeeper David Jones to score for Hull City in a 2-0 win at Boothferry Park in October 1958.

Brian Bulless, a versatile player with one of the best left feet in the club's history, recalled: "There was a bit of unrest in the early part of the season although I can't really remember what caused it. We scored goals regularly thanks in the main to Bill Bradbury and Colin Smith although they got some good support from some of the others. Doug Clarke had joined us as an inside-forward, but he must have been one of the best right-wingers the club ever had and he used to score plenty of goals, too. All-round we may not have been a great side, but we had a lot of team spirit and that was very important to us."

Bulless's teammate Colin Smith, who was later to travel the world as a soccer coach, agreed: "I really enjoyed my time with City as a player. One of the differences in those days was that everybody lived in the area and we were with each other most of the time. The club had about 40 professionals and socially we moved around with each other far more." In those days, for example, City players frequently attended greyhound meetings at Craven Park in Hull and one story goes that Doug Clarke once gave his teammates a hot tip straight from the kennels. They duly backed the dog, which is then supposed to have dropped dead during the race although Clarke himself insists: "I probably wished it had, but it didn't!"

Doug Clarke beats Accrington Stanley's goalkeeper Willie McInnes, one of the many Scots in their side in those days, during Hull City's 4-2 win at Boothferry Park in September 1958.

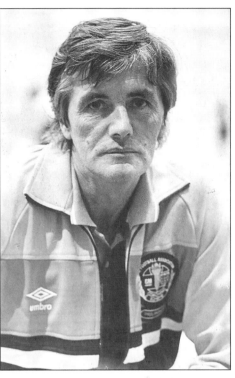

Bill Bradbury, who died in August 1999, had an exceptional goalscoring record throughout his stay with the Tigers: he was also a great character. He once dressed up in groundsman Stan Coombs' cap, muffler and coat and drove his mower round the pitch in the fog to avoid training. Manager Bob Brocklebank even said:"Hello, Stan" to him as he went past! Another incident during a match would probably have registered on the Eric Cantona scale nowadays. "There was a small home crowd and someone was having a go at me as I went to take a corner, so I threw the ball at him. It hit him on the nose, I saw his eyes start to water and the ball came straight back to me. I put it down and scored straight from the corner!" said Bradbury. He also subscribed to the "all-for-one and one-for-all" theory to explain the 1958-59 promotion campaign: "The club looked after us very well. Nothing was too much trouble for them and I was treated like a king. They were great times when we won promotion because Hull City were a very friendly club and we had a smashing team spirit. We may not have been a great footballing side, but we didn't have many injuries and we just went out and enjoyed ourselves. There weren't any small groups of players – we went everywhere together and we had lots of laughs and a hell of a time."

Skipper Paul Feasey, a dominant centre-half despite being a little less than 5ft. 9in. tall, was an inspirational figure that season and he pointed to the training conditions as a factor in the success. He said:"We always used to maintain that it helped us a lot when we trained on the club car-park. It made such a difference to train on the ash because it was lighter going all the time and it was never any effort for us to get through

Paul Feasey, Hull City's defensive rock during the promotion campaign of 1958-59, beats Rochdale's Tom McGlennon in a 2-1 win at Boothferry Park in April 1959.

Hull City's goalkeeper Maurice Swan gets the club's high-scoring forward-line in his camera sights during a break in training in March 1966. They are (left to right): Ray Henderson, Ken Wagstaff, Chris Chilton, Ken Houghton, Ian Butler.

Ray Henderson heads a first-minute goal for Hull City against Scunthorpe United in a 4-2 victory at the Old Showground in January 1966. Teammates Chris Chilton (left) and Ken Wagstaff get a close-up of it.

games as far as fitness was concerned. It was also blood-and-thunder training. We'd split up into five-a-side teams and have a bit of a league with the losers having to buy the Mars Bars for the winners at Billy Bly's sweet shop near the ground!"

The 1965-66 season dawned amid a growing expectation that the Tigers would win promotion. The investments of the previous season – Ken Wagstaff, Ian Butler and Ken Houghton, who had all been signed for £40,000 to complement the exceptional Chris Chilton – had given the side a potent and creative forward-line by most standards, never mind the Third Division. Having just missed out in 1964-65, City were expected to produce the goods and went into the season as one of the favourites for promotion. Success was almost a foregone conclusion provided that the Tigers carried on where they had finished off in the second half of 1964-65 and did not suffer a major hangover as a result of just missing out.

They started brightly enough by taking seven points out of the first eight, but were then brought back down to earth with two successive home defeats – 3-1 against Queen's Park Rangers and 4-1 against York City. The side could score goals almost at will, but they were conceding more than they might have anticipated. And although the team were virtually to pick themselves for most of the season, there were some notable changes in the early part of the season. Maurice Swan became the regular goalkeeper in place of Mike Williams, Ray Henderson commanded the problem outside-right berth after Billy Wilkinson and Terry Heath had initially been

tried in it and Gerry Summers, more recently a leading light in Derby County's youth development programme, was sold to Walsall and Alan Jarvis took his place.

Jarvis made his League debut in amusing circumstances in October 1965. The week before he was given his chance, City's reserves were winning a game so easily that Ron Rafferty and Billy Wilkinson bet Jarvis £2 at halftime that he did not dare to sit on the ball during play. Jarvis did do and won the bet, but was fined £5 by the club and then promoted to the first team immediately! "I'd got pig-sick of playing in the reserves at the time," he once told me.

In all, City were to play 55 games that season and they scored in all but three of them – when they lost 3-0 at Workington, 3-0 at Millwall and 1-0 at Grimsby Town in the League. They accumulated 122 goals overall and the fans were spoilt because

Hull City's Chris Chilton, watched by his teammate Ian Butler, heads past Bournemouth's goal-keeper David Best to score in a 3-0 victory at Boothferry Park in October 1965.

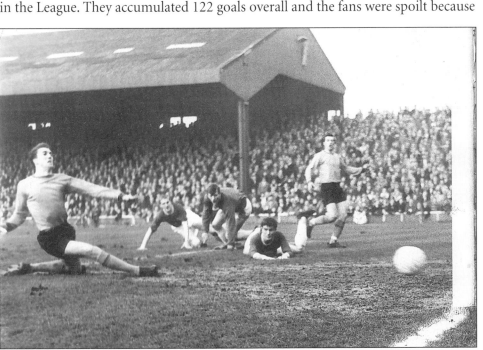

Ian Butler (right) leaves the Exeter City defence in his wake to set up one of Hull City centre-forward Chris Chilton's goals in his hat-trick in a 6-1 win at Boothferry Park in April 1966.

Hull City's Chris Chilton outjumps Walsall's defender Stan Bennett to head home in a 3-2 win at Boothferry Park in October 1965.

they were watching not only a successful side, but also a memorably entertaining one who could basically score goals at will. They set club records for 109 League goals in a season and 45 League goals on their travels. They had five different players in double figures for League goals for the first time, having failed by just one goal to achieve the feat in both 1948-49 and 1956-57. They scored six at home to Bristol Rovers, Workington and Exeter City, while Wagstaff scored four himself at Brentford, Chilton recorded hat-tricks at home to Oldham Athletic and Exeter and Ian Butler hit one at Walsall.

The Tigers won ten consecutive League games at one stage and even set an attendance record for the Third Division in its non-regional format when they entertained promotion rivals Millwall on Boxing Day, 1965, in front of a 40,231 crowd. Aston Villa later broke the crowd record, but City won 1-0 thanks to an untidy own goal accredited to John Gilchrist as Wagstaff put him under pressure. Millwall's side that day included Tom Wilson, who later served the Tigers in a variety of roles such as assistant manager, reserve coach and secretary, and he recalled: "We'd had a bad journey to Hull by train, but it was a tremendous sight when the bus taking us to the ground got near Boothferry Park. There were about ten or 12 queues at the front of the ground, stretching right across the car-park. The fans were standing side by side laughing and joking and it was a big lift to us after our journey. The match itself was spoilt by the pitch because it was bone-hard. It was very

Queues form as 40,231 fans prepare to watch Hull City's Boxing Day clash with promotion rivals Millwall at Boothferry Park in 1965.

Hull City's centre-half Mick Milner heads the ball back to goalkeeper Maurice Swan as skipper Andy Davidson watches on the line in the 1-0 win over close rivals Millwall on Boxing Day 1965. The Lions' Len Julians and Hugh Curran apply the pressure in the Tigers' goalmouth.

grassy, but had a shiny look about it and, as the game wore on, it became more like a skating-rink. After the match the two teams travelled to London together for the return fixture. We both went by train from Hessle, but had to have police escorts to the station because of the size of the crowd."

City's lowest home gate that season was 12,440 against Bournemouth and they clinched promotion on the night of May 6, 1966 when they won 2-1 at Bristol Rovers. It was appropriate because manager Cliff Britton was a Bristolian by birth and Rovers were his first club as a player. It was also ironic that only a little more than ten years earlier he had said that he was finished with soccer for good when his eight-year stint in charge of Everton ended. But it turned out nicely again for him with the Tigers and he said of that memorable campaign: "The season was one of the finest of my career and what made it so was the team's devotion to teamwork – the very essence of soccer – and the high degree of consistency with which we have carried out the plans we have laid down for them. My theory is that what happens on a match day is a reflection of what has gone on in training during the week when

Hull City's goalkeeper Maurice Swan pounces on the ball before Bristol Rovers' Roger Frude on the night that Hull City made sure of promotion with a 2-1 victory at Eastville in May 1966. The Tigers' Mick Milner (left) and Alan Jarvis keep a close watch on the proceedings, while their colleague Dennis Butler guards the line.

Hull City's manager Cliff Britton (left) with the club's board after the 1-0 win over Southend United that clinched the Third Division title in May 1966. The directors are (left to right): John Needler, Geoffrey Rignall, Stan Kershaw, Harold Needler, Henry Needler and Ron Buttery.

you plan, practise, try to make improvements and iron out faults. And everyone has approached the task in a fine spirit, cutting out any tendency to be individualistic and accept a general pattern of play. There has been particular proof of this in the way in which the goals have been shared out. I don't think there is another forward-line in the country in which the goals have been spread out so evenly and so thickly."

Chris Chilton, City's leading goalscorer of all time, took the philosophy a stage further when he reflected: "I think Cliff knew that he had strikers who would score goals, but there was tremendous loyalty among those players to the club and to each other. We also had respect for the manager and everything was governed by that. I think they were possibly glory days. Certainly everybody knew all the players and we were never put on a pedestal on the financial side. We were just ordinary working blokes. And when we played, the majority of us were on the same kind of wage

Cliff Britton, Hull City's promotion-winning manager in 1965-66.

level as the people who were watching us, so that always quashed any thoughts of resentment. When we were playing, we never felt sure that we would always be in the side from one week to the next and nothing was taken for granted. Too many people expect things to happen to them nowadays, but in any walk of life you always have to have a target."

The players of that era generally respected Cliff Britton for his thoroughness and methodical attention to detail and skipper Andy Davidson said:"He was immaculate in everything he did and worked everything out with a fine tooth-comb." Britton could also be a strict disciplinarian and full-back Dennis Butler recalled: "You couldn't help but look up to him. Cliff went into

Hull City's Chris Chilton steers the ball past Peterborough United's goalkeeper Willie Duff in the 2-1 home win in May 1966.

Hull City's Ken Houghton coolly places the ball past Watford's goalkeeper Bobby Slater in their 3-1 home win in November 1965.

every detail about things and he was also a gentleman and a teetotaller. I can remember my first game at Watford when the other players were drinking ginger beer or milk or orange squash and I had a cider. Gus McLean, the coach, told me: 'Make that your first and last because this is a teetotal outfit' and he meant it!"

It was to be a long while with more troughs than peaks before the Tigers were to achieve promotion again. Mike Smith's reign as manager was not particularly successful and the club found themselves in the Fourth Division in 1981 and in receivership early in 1982. The financial crisis ended Smith's spell in charge, but, to be fair to him, he did at least leave behind a squad of players who might be capable of going on to better things.

Colin Appleton, who had worked closely with new chairman Don Robinson as manager of his home-town club Scarborough as the two of them turned them into one of the country's top non-League clubs, merely honed them to good effect

Hull City's promotion-winning defender Dennis Butler.

Hull City's promotion regulars in 1965-66. Back row (left to right): Dennis Butler, Alan Jarvis, Andy Davidson, Maurice Swan, Mick Milner, Chris Simpkin; front row, Ray Henderson, Ken Wagstaff, Chris Chilton, Ken Houghton, Ian Butler.

when he took charge. He had to work on a shoestring budget after the trauma of receivership in the early part of 1982, but he was worldly-wise and thoroughly experienced in soccer terms.

City's second season in the Fourth Division did not begin too promisingly, though, as they won only twice in their first eight League games. But Appleton adjusted well to having to work within strict financial constraints, he made the most of what he did have and the Tigers were notoriously difficult to beat. They lost only five more League games after their indifferent opening, but each time they bounced

Hull City's successful chairman Don Robinson.

back straightaway to put together another useful unbeaten run. They won four out of four between two defeats, they then won five and drew two out of seven, they were undefeated in ten matches in a two-month period early in 1983 and then won four and drew two out of six as promotion could be seen on the horizon.

It came in a goalless draw at Chester on April 30, 1983, and City finished as the runners-up in the Fourth Division to Wimbledon, who amassed 98 points. Following the Tigers on 90 were Port Vale with 88 and Scunthorpe United with 83 and they were also promoted. City lost only one home

League game – 1-0 to Tranmere Rovers – and conceded the fewest home goals – 14. They and Port Vale gave away the fewest goals throughout the season – just 34.

Colin Appleton had achieved success with only minor alterations to the squad whom he had inherited. He brought popular defender Peter Skipper, the only ever-present that season, back to the club from Darlington for £10,000 with the aid of the fans' own generosity and the left-sided Billy Askew had joined City on trial, established himself in the side and was to prove to be one of the most shrewd free-transfer signings ever. Other than that, Appleton introduced striker Billy Woof, who had been a teammate of Askew at Middlesbrough, as a useful squad member, brought striker John Hawley back to Boothferry Park on loan and signed former England international Emlyn Hughes after his spell as Rotherham United's manager had ended. Hughes was born in Barrow, where Appleton had been player-manager in their days as a League club in the late 1960s. The link between the two went that far back.

Brian Marwood was the top goalscorer in the League on 19 and he received good support from Les Mutrie and Andy Flounders, but Appleton basically worked miracles, made sure that the side were always well-organised and turned unsuccessful players into successful ones. He was a deep thinker on the game and if he sometimes appeared to talk in riddles, he would still come out with moments of great common-sense and perception and with a way of viewing things that no-one else had thought about. He believed in a strong work ethic, in-depth pre-match meetings and a healthy banter in the dressing-room. Appleton earned respect in 1982-83 although the public often underrated him, but listening to his philosophies on the game remains a joy.

It was generally felt that the uncertainty that had been created by the club's spell in receivership had been turned into a positive ion and Dennis Booth, another great character in the dressing-room who was with City as a player and coach for almost nine years, recalled: "It was a complete turnaround after the traumas of receivership. But I remember that when Mike Smith and Cyril Lea left and Bobby Brown and Chris Chilton became caretaker managers the previous season, we got the spirit going then and we all mucked in together. We all pulled together and became stronger in adversity, so that when Colin Appleton took over, the spirit was already there. We already had the nucleus of a good side and Colin just built on it. He was always well-organised and knew what he wanted. He liked to juggle the team about, probably as a guard against complacency, and we didn't have any idea of what he might be thinking at times, but he liked to have a lot of attacking players around the place and he made us an attractive side to watch."

Hull City's long-serving player and coach Dennis Booth.

The proof came in the latter part of the season when Flounders scored a hat-trick in a 7-0 win at home to Stockport County – a game which drew different reactions from skipper Garreth Roberts and Dennis Booth. Roberts said:"The way we were playing at the time typified the togetherness and camaraderie between all the lads after our horrendous feelings when the receiver was called in. To have been at the club and not known just what was going on was very unsettling at the time, but this win probably proved just how well we'd all done to bounce back and work for each other." But Booth amusingly insisted: "It was one of the most boring games I played in during my career. We were 4-0 up in the first half-hour, we knew the goals were going to go in and some of us just didn't have anything to do. I seem to remember that Stockport went and got a very good result the following week, which often seems to happen in such circumstances."

Booth, whose promotion-laden playing career was once crowned by a hat-trick of headers in one game for Lincoln City even though he is only 5ft. 8in. tall, also stressed how well the Tigers team of 1982-83 did when the chips were really down against their promotion rivals: "We had a few days at Scarborough and basically just had a good time before going to Scunthorpe for a night match, but we won 1-0 with a goal by Les Mutrie, who was a good player in that side and should have played at a higher level. Then we came back after one of our rare defeats to win 2-1 at Wimbledon and Dale Roberts got the winner in the last few seconds of the game. Then we beat Port Vale at home in front of a crowd of almost 15,000. Emlyn Hughes made his debut in midfield and said he was shattered by the end of the match. We always felt we were going to go up, but the way we played in some of big games proved it and showed what a good side we had."

And Booth also put it all in a wider context because he added: "Don Robinson was in his element as our chairman, but both Hull FC and Hull Kingston Rovers were also doing well in rugby league and the city as a whole was buzzing. It was a very special time in Hull for everyone."

After just missing out on a second successive promotion, hopes were high in 1984-85 in the same way as they had been back in 1965-66 because in both instances City were expected to do well after just being pipped for promotion the previous season. Brian Horton, whose League career had taken him to Port Vale, Brighton and Hove Albion and Luton Town, took over as player-manager following Colin Appleton's departure to Swansea City. He was new to management, but he had established a reputation for himself as a formidable leader as a player and he was to play in almost half his side's League games on the road to promotion. It is a curi-

ous, but little-known fact, though, that it was Appleton who had paved the way for Horton to come to Boothferry Park because he had wanted to sign him as a player: the irony was in the way in which it actually happened.

City did not make a particularly good start to the season and again won only two of their opening eight League games, but then they lost only one of the next 16, including a 13-match unbeaten run up to the end of January. February was not a good month because it brought only one League victory in five games, but Brian Horton had signed defender Richard Jobson from Watford for £40,000 to strengthen his squad and the Tigers again cruised into top gear. March brought five successive wins and six victories and a draw in seven games in total. City were to lose only one game in 15 – 2-0 at Bristol City on Easter Monday – and there was another sequence of five victories in a row,

Brian Horton, Hull City's player-manager when they won promotion in 1984-85.

the last of which brought them promotion when they won 1-0 at Walsall on May 4, 1985, with a goal by Peter Skipper.

City finished third on 87 points behind Millwall on 90 and champions Bradford City on 94 and they were the second highest goalscorers in the division with 78 – two fewer than fourth-placed Gillingham. Billy Whitehurst had become a prolific marksman and was the top scorer in the League with 20 goals, while Andy Flounders and defender Stan McEwan also chipped in with valuable contributions.

Horton had been an instant success in management and he was to prove popular with the fans. If anything, his influence and beliefs gained greater credence with

Hull City's promotion squad of 1984-85. Back row (left to right): Gary Swann, Paul Olsson, Andy Flounders, Lawrie Pearson, Bobby McNeil, Ian Davis, Neil Williams; middle row, Chris Chilton (assistant manager), Mick Hollifield, John Davies, Billy Whitehurst, Tony Norman, Stan McEwan, Peter Skipper, Dennis Booth (player-coach); front row, Dale Roberts, Steve Massey, Garreth Roberts, Brian Horton (player-manager), Don Robinson (chairman), Steve McClaren, Billy Askew, Jeff Radcliffe (physiotherapist).

the public in hindsight after he had been sacked by Don Robinson with undue haste in April 1988. He had an eye for bargain signings, he built a solid foundation and he was a determined, driven competitor who could not always accept anything less than winning too comfortably. Horton and his predecessor Colin Appleton had very different styles of management, but they were both decent, honest hard-working football people who brought the Tigers some badly-needed success.

And while Horton had earned promotion in his first season in management, coach Chris Chilton had helped the Tigers to their second promotion in three years to go with the one that he had enjoyed as a player in 1965-66. Midfield player Garreth Roberts, meanwhile, became the first player to captain two City promotion teams and he reflected: "Even though it was Brian's first managerial job, he first met us when he came out to Florida, where we'd gone at the end of the season. He took us for training and it was a great way for him to get to know the lads because we needed picking up after just missing out. Brian basically took up the slack and I think he knew were still a good enough team to do well. He made a few changes here and there, but he made sure that we went out on to the park feeling that nobody could beat us, especially at home. Everybody was working for each other and I think that Brian may compare that team favourably with any he's managed since. From a personal point of view, it helped that he was also a midfield player and he never surrendered to anyone, even in training sessions, which got a bit lively and tasty at times!"

The success of the 1980s can be attributed in no small part to the dynamism of chairman Don Robinson, a Scarborough-based entertainments entrepreneur. His personality lit up Boothferry Park, he came out with some outrageous comments and stunts and there was seldom a dull moment while he was around. He may have acted hurriedly at times, but he was full of ideas: he always courted popularity with the public, but he went out of his way to liaise with the fans and keep their belief and zest as intact as his own. At times it was possible to fall out with him, but he never bore grudges: the gravest threat came when he was displeased with you and would grab you in a head-lock that was a throwback to his days as a top-class wrestler known as Dr Death. It brought a new meaning to the term Robinson's squash…

Garreth Roberts has no doubt about Don Robinson's character and charisma as he transformed City's fortunes: "Don was the best chairman I worked under. He was great for the club at the time because he was just what was needed. I thought he was brilliant – a top man. Some of his quotes at the time about City being the first side to play on the moon were just plain daft and you wouldn't say that kind of thing nowadays. It was dead easy for people to take the mickey out of us after that, but it was Don's way of letting them know what a good team we were. He used to take us abroad for trips and up to Scarborough for a few days to keep us all together and he'd get us involved in all kinds of stunts. I can remember him getting me to feed some dolphins on one occasion. He told muggins to stand there with a fish in my teeth and this dolphin with its mouth wide open suddenly jumped up and took it. Can you imagine David Beckham doing that nowadays?"

Don Robinson has since tried to return to the Boothferry Park boardroom, but he has repeatedly been rebuffed, often by directors with whom he had shared a place on the board. Maybe they were envious of his success, but there was to be no more of it without him between 1985 and the end of the 20th century. Rather the opposite, in fact…

Chapter Eight

Down, Down

THE mere fact that Hull City are seeing out the 20th century in the present Third Division or what was for many years the old Fourth Division proves one point – they have had more relegations than promotions in their history. The statistic is quite simply a direct indictment of their capacity for flattering to deceive.

For much of the century they did not go either up or down very much at all. That led to its own anti-climax, but, frustrating though that pattern might have been, it was more digestible than what has gone in the latter years of the 20th century. In 1981 they went down to that Fourth Division for the first time ever, but they bounced back after just two seasons. Since then, they have gone down into its equivalent – the Third Division – and have ended up being there a bit longer. Quite simply, they are ending the 20th century in their worst-ever state according to League status.

City's first-ever relegation came in deeply ironic circumstances. They had always retained their status in the old Second Division with reasonable comfort since they first became a League club and had already underlined their reputation and promise with a series of FA Cup giantkilling acts. Two of them occurred in the 1929-30 season as City reached the semi-finals for the only time in their history. But the Tigers ended having to face up to far more than missing out on a Wembley date: they also had to suffer the bathos of relegation at the end of the season.

Everything had started so optimistically as City won four – Welshman Ken McDonald scored in all of them – and drew one of their opening five games. But they won only one of their next ten League games before winning four out of the next six up to Christmas Day. Twice that season the Tigers lost four League games on the trot and the second time it was part of a sequence of only one win in 12. By April 1930 City's FA Cup hopes had disappeared and the possibility of relegation was becoming increasingly real. In addition, Stan Alexander had regularly been among the goals, but they were beginning to dry up from all sources.

A few days after the FA Cup semi-final exit against Arsenal in a replay, City beat

Oldham Athletic 1-0 at home with a goal by Joe Murray. But then a disastrous run of six games in April 1930 produced just one point out of 12, including a 7-1 trouncing at West Bromwich Albion, admittedly the division's top scorers. The Tigers had the cushion of knowing that their last three games were at home, including a vital clash with fellow strugglers Bristol City, but injuries were disrupting them at a crucial stage of the season and they slipped into the relegation zone.

City lost at Bradford City and Bury, who were then involved in a bribes scandal concerning a match between each other, but beat Tottenham Hotspur 2-1 at Anlaby Road as the injury situation abated. The next twist, though, brought a Mayday signal in 1930: the Tigers lost 1-0 at home to Bristol City on May 1 and found themselves at the bottom of the table. As it was, Notts County were to finish at the bottom, but Bristol City earned their salvation at Preston on the final day when the Tigers' 2-0 home win over Wolverhampton Wanderers with goals by Alexander was not enough to save them. City went down at Bristol City's expense by one-twelfth of a goal because both finished on the same number of points and they and their fans mused on an incident near the end of the vital game between the two when a shot by Stan Dixon hit the underside of the bar and appeared to drop over the line. Presumably Russian linesmen had not yet been invented and that was the difference between success and failure for City, whose manager Bill McCracken reflected: "Luck has been dead against us of late and to go down on goal average is the last straw."

After their first promotion campaign back to the Second Division in 1932-33, City had two respectable mid-table seasons. Haydn Green resigned as manager in March 1934 and Jack Hill, the former England centre-half whom he had signed, was a unanimous choice as his successor. Hill retired as a player and began a rebuilding process that involved a big turnover of players, eventually including an influx of Scots. But injuries and illnesses took their toll in 1935-36 when 32 different players were used and the Tigers slowly found themselves on a slippery slope. Jack Acquroff and Cliff Woodhead played in all but one of the 42 League games, but there was never a settled side.

The Tigers won only four of their opening 19 League games – all of them at home – and then lost six in a row in a two-month spell from mid-December, beginning with a 7-0 thrashing at Sheffield United. City's only away win of the season came at Plymouth Argyle in February 1936 when Acquroff scored the only goal of the game, but they did not win any of their remaining 16 games.

Crowds slumped disastrously: there had been 11,657 fans at the first home game against Fulham when the club's new blue-and-white colours were first unveiled, but the game against Leicester Fosse at Anlaby Road at the end of February 1936 attracted what was then a record low gate of 2,284. A month earlier, though, Hill had resigned as manager and David Menzies, who had previously been in charge of City between 1916 and 1921, was brought back as his successor, but he could do little to stop the rot.

The Tigers' goalscoring record was not great although Southampton survived comfortably enough in the Second Division that season by scoring the same number – 47. Jack Acquroff and Ken Cameron had respectable returns, but only twice did City score more than twice in a game. The defensive record, however, was debilitating. In addition to the hammering at Sheffield United, the Tigers conceded six at Doncaster Rovers and Swansea Town and five against Barnsley and Bradford City. In all, City gave away 111 League goals – the joint worst tally nationally that season with Third Division South strugglers Newport County – in obtaining just 20 points. And that left them a prodigious 12 points adrift of Port Vale, with whom they were relegated.

Twenty years later City again went down from the Second Division and it was probably not a great surprise even though Bob Brocklebank, who had replaced Bob Jackson in controversial circumstances in March 1955, was at the helm for his first full season in charge. City had had a series of disappointing seasons and in 1955-56 they were relegated.

The Tigers simply never fully recovered from a terrible start to the season in which they won only one of their opening 15 games. During the autumn Brocklebank started to ring the changes and made three notable signings – Bill Bradbury, Doug Clarke and former England centre-forward Stan Mortensen. Bradbury scored on his debut even though City lost 3-2 at home to Bury: a month later he scored his second goal for the club in a 3-1 home win over West Ham United, in which Clarke and Mortensen were also on the mark on their debuts. It began a more optimistic run of four victories in six games, but it was a false dawn because the Tigers then lost five of the following six.

There was again a big turnover of personnel and Andy Davidson was easily the only-ever present that season. And again there were defensive frailties that were to leave City with the worst record in the top two divisions because they conceded 97 goals in the League. There were only four clean sheets, two of them against fellow strugglers Notts County. The fourth came at Rotherham in a 2-0 win in which Dave Fraser scored twice on his first-team debut. Fraser, who was to score the Tigers' last goal on a Christmas Day in 1957, brought a ray of light to the dismal end-of-season proceedings by grabbing a total of six goals in the last six games. But relegation was confirmed in a 1-1 draw at home to Doncaster Rovers under floodlights immediately after the triumph at Rotherham. As if there were some sort of relief for being put out of their misery, the Tigers at once responded by recording their biggest win of the season when they defeated Barnsley 4-1 at Boothferry Park.

But a 5-1 thrashing at Middlesbrough followed and then City had to endure a 4-1 home defeat against Leeds United in a galling situation in their penultimate match of the season. Inspired by John Charles, Leeds were on their way to the First Division as runners-up to Sheffield Wednesday. The Tigers probably wanted to close the season on as anonymous a note as possible, but there was a crowd of 31,123 at Boothferry Park. It was City's biggest home gate of a disappointing season, but they got their anonymity three days later when just 5,232 turned up for the last rites in a 3-2 win over Stoke City at Boothferry Park…

In 1959-60, the Tigers found that what went up came straight down. Having been promoted as runners-up to Plymouth Argyle in the first season of the non-regional Third Division in 1958-59, they could not cope with the higher level. They finished in 21st place and went down with Bristol City after taking only 30 points. It was two more than Bristol City, but they were still three behind Portsmouth. They struggled to score goals and managed only 48 – the lowest tally in the Second Division that season.

Hull City's Ralph Gubbins, watched by his teammate Roy Shiner, finds space to beat Brighton and Hove Albion's defender Roy Jennings to head home in a 3-1 win at Boothferry Park in November 1959.

Ironically, they began the season with a 3-1 win over Plymouth – an improvement on a year earlier when they opened their programme with the corresponding fixture and drew only 1-1. Former England left-winger Vic Metcalfe made his debut in the first game and did not play for the club again until the second when he promptly scored twice. But it was a false dawn because City lost their next five games and gave away 21 goals in the process. After winning 1-0 at Bristol City, they went eight games without another win and manager Bob Brocklebank tried to change things for the better by introducing a lot more experience into the forward-line – former England international Jackie Sewell, who had been the costliest player in the country when he cost Sheffield Wednesday £34,500 in March 1951, from Aston Villa, Roy Shiner from Sheffield Wednesday and Ralph Gubbins from Bolton Wanderers.

Hull City's Roy Shiner outjumps Sunderland's popular defender Charlie Hurley in a goalless draw at Boothferry Park in April 1960. Watching are Sunderland's Reg Pearce (left) and Ernie Taylor and City's Les Collinson.

Bill Bradbury scores the first of his two goals in a 3-3 draw at home to Middlesbrough in September 1959. Watching are 'Boro defenders Brian Phillips (left) and Ray Bilcliff.

They cost a total of £14,000, but although Shiner scored twice on his debut in a 3-1 home win over Bristol Rovers, the Tigers were on the slide and they could not prevent it from happening.

City won only once – 1-0 at home to Rotherham United in a 12-match sequence between mid-December and mid-March and the writing was on the wall. And in February 1960 Bill Bradbury, whose goals had guided the club to promotion the previous season, moved on to Bury in a £5,000 deal – £1,000 more than the Tigers had paid for him from Birmingham City in October 1955. Strangely, youngster Dave King had scored twice on his League debut in a 3-1 win at Sunderland in December 1959, played in the next game and was then overlooked for much of the rest of the season. Remarkably, though, when he was finally given another chance, City finished the season by remaining unbeaten in their final seven games and King scored five times in them.

It all came too late, though, and a Hull City era ended just as that final undefeated run began. Billy Bly, the club's long-serving goalkeeper who had joined them in August 1937, played his final game and was unceremoniously released at the end of the season. The end came in a 1-0 defeat at Bristol Rovers on March 26, 1960, but the ever-popular Bly had clocked up 403 League appearances for City – a figure

Dave King, whose goals could not save Hull City in 1959-60.

that would have been far higher if it had not been for the interruption caused by World War Two and a host of serious injuries from which he had repeatedly bounced back to defy the odds. Bob Brocklebank, meanwhile, had become the first City manager to take the club down twice.

As in 1929-30, City had had a long spell in the Second Division without ever consistently looking as if they might go either up or down when the 1977-78 season dawned. Hopes were high, though, because the Tigers had former Scotland captain Billy Bremner, current

Welsh international Dave Roberts, future Northern Ireland winger Dave Stewart and England under-21 internationals Paul Haigh and Peter Daniel in their ranks. They began the season with a stirring 3-0 win over Sunderland in front of 16,189 fans at Boothferry Park. It was to be the highest home crowd of the season and a false dawn. The season was to descend into one of change and a lack of stability that was undermine the original expectations for it.

City won only two of their opening eight League games and in the last game in the sequence they had lost 2-0 at home to Mansfield Town, who were playing in the Second Division for the first time. On the morning of the match manager John Kaye had had an altercation with director Bob Chapman on the telephone: by the end of it he had been sacked straightaway by chairman Christopher Needler, who promptly went away on holiday! Former Scotland, Everton and Leeds United hero Bobby Collins, who had joined the club as first-team coach in the summer of 1977 as the successor to Phil Holme, was appointed as caretaker manager.

Collins and Billy Bremner, arguably teacher and pupil respectively as Leeds developed into a major force under the management of ex-Tiger Don Revie, found themselves competing for the managerial vacancy. In Collins' first game in temporary charge the Tigers beat Tottenham Hotspur 2-0 at home with goals by Alan Warboys and they took five points out of six. It was enough to earn Collins the manager's job on a long-term basis, but it led to a rift between him and the overlooked Bremner. Collins did his best to be reasonable, but his honeymoon period

Hull City's Alan Warboys scores his first goal for the club in a 2-0 home win over Tottenham Hotspur at Boothferry Park in October 1977. Spurs' goalkeeper Barry Daines and centre-half Keith Osgood can only watch in vain.

Hull City's Dave Stewart beats Cardiff City's goalkeeper Bill Irwin to score in the first minute of a 4-1 home win in November 1977.

was over. His demanding standards brought about by a fervent desire to win at all times meant that he publicly criticised his players when they beat Cardiff City 4-1 at home. The next nine League games brought a response of six defeats and three draws.

Collins opted to bring in a fellow Footballer of the Year, Syd Owen, as his No. 2 in preference to Ken Houghton, who was already on the backroom staff. Owen, a former England defender, had been largely responsible for compiling manager Don Revie's famed dossiers on opposition sides at Leeds United. He was utterly passionate about football, but he was strait-laced and serious and may have been a little out of touch with the players of a younger generation. The partnership did not work well in practice even though Collins had some excellent ideas in theory: furthermore, he had to deal with a new chairman. Christopher Needler resigned just after Christmas 1977 and his successor was Bob Chapman. An exceedingly-pleasant, outgoing man with a ready handshake, he developed a penchant for trawling through soccer yearbooks to judge players on their ratio of goals scored to the number of appearances – and not much more. It was part of his all-round enthusiasm, but it soon waned for Bobby Collins and Syd Owen and he sacked them both in February 1978, putting Ken Houghton in caretaker charge. Collins had been City manager for almost two seasons – autumn and winter!

Alan Warboys immediately came up with the goods again in Houghton's first home match in charge when he scored a hat-trick in a 3-2 win over Millwall, but City won only one of their final 13 League games of the season – 1-0 at Charlton Athletic. When they returned to London a fortnight later – on April 22, 1978, Warboys again scored, but City lost 2-1 and were condemned to relegation to the old Third Division.

Ken Houghton did well in his first full season in charge when City finished eighth in the Third Division in 1978-79, but the following season he was sacked by Bob Chapman and replaced with Mike Smith. City nearly went down to the Fourth

Hull City's short-lived management team of Bobby Collins (left) and Syd Owen during the 1977-78 season.

Division, but it was only a temporary stay of execution. They were to go down again in 1980-81 – Smith's own first full season in charge.

It was a disappointing campaign from the outset as the Tigers won only one of their opening 17 League games – 2-1 at home to Portsmouth – up to the end of October 1980. In that period City went nine League games without a win, lost seven in succession, scored only one goal in eight and went five without a goal.

Furthermore, there was an autumn sale when former England under-21 international defender Paul Haigh moved to Carlisle United in a £100,000 deal. Nearer Christmas, the reliable full-back Gordon Nisbet, a former England under-23 international and a popular figure with the public, was sold to Plymouth Argyle for £30,000. Later in the season another defender, Stuart Croft, joined Portsmouth, while Smith's revolution meant that there were plenty of new faces as Billy Whitehurst, Les Mutrie, Brian Ferguson, Steve Hoolickin and Stuart Eccleston all became regular members of the side. Whether there were too many changes of personnel too soon is open to debate: things were going from bad to worse. Smith had brought in some useful players, some of them on high wages for the Third Division, but at that time they did not gel. Keith Edwards, for example, was comfortably the top goalscorer with 13 in the League, but he caused a stir by throwing his shirt at the home dug-out after he had been controversially substituted in a goalless draw with Brentford at Boothferry Park in February 1981.

Attendances slumped to just a little more than 3,000 on a regular basis and two successive wins early in 1981 – 3-1 at Exeter City and 2-1 at home to Blackpool – only put off the inevitable because a further sequence of 11 games without a win immediately followed. The success at Exeter provided the only away win of the season, but six games from the end of it the Tigers drew 0-0 at home to Swindon Town and it was not enough to save them from the drop. Their worst fears were confirmed and it all coincided with a protest from a recently-formed Hull City Action Group, who were to create greater consternation in the early part of the following season then they carried a coffin to Boothferry Park as a sign of the death of the club.

A little annoyingly the Tigers then took three points out of four against promotion-chasing Huddersfield Town and Rotherham United and then they irritated another Yorkshire club, Sheffield United, by holding them to a 1-1 draw at Boothferry Park. A win would ultimately have saved the Blades from emulating City by dropping into the Fourth Division for the first time in their history, but they also went down with Blackpool and Colchester United. The Tigers finished at the bottom of the Third Division and they and Blackpool were seven points adrift of Colchester. It was hardly surprising, therefore, that only 2,059 fans saw the last game of the season – a 3-1 home win over Newport County – as they prepared for Fourth Division soccer for the first time ever.

The 1980s brought a revival under Don Robinson's extrovert chairmanship, but the 1990s were to prove even more disconcerting for City fans. All the good work was thrown away and the Tigers were to return to the bottom flight of English League soccer in even more desperate circumstances.

Everything started to turn sour in 1990-91 when City went down to the old Third Division. Manager Stan Ternent had done well to save the club from impending disaster after taking over during the previous season and there were grounds for optimism although the side generally did not play well on their pre-season tour of Bulgaria, during which they crucially lost influential defender Malcolm Shotton with a hernia problem. The Tigers failed to win any of their opening seven League games, during which Ternent found himself without another important defender when he was forced to sell Richard Jobson to Oldham Athletic. A 7-1 hammering against West Ham United at Upton Park underlined the defensive frailties, but there was also a 5-2 home win over Leicester City towards the end of November 1990.

The following month the long-serving Garreth Roberts played his last League game before being forced to retire because of knee trouble, but Ternent and chairman Richard Chetham had had a policy disagreement in the early part of the campaign and City were at the bottom of the table by the end of 1990. The parting of the ways occurred amid a seven-match run without a win and followed a 5-1 defeat at Portsmouth on January 3, 1990, by which the Tigers had won only five League games out of 25, but, curiously enough, they had scored 40 goals. They were leaking them rather alarmingly, however, although most of the players with the club at that time felt that City would have tightened up and subsequently stayed up if Ternent had stayed. As it was, the axe fell on him after just 14 months at the helm as he became just another short-serving manager in the club's history. Directors seldom admit a mistake publicly, but it is always amazing how someone can be the right man for a job one instant and then the wrong man for it so comparatively soon afterwards. In such instances the buck should surely stop with the person who made the appointment in the first place.

Ultimately, Chetham brought in Terry Dolan as Ternent's successor: it was pure Hull City irony that the two of them had worked with each other as a handy management team at Bradford City. Furthermore, they had been sacked after the Tigers had beaten Bradford City 2-1 at Valley Parade in the FA Cup's fourth round in 1988-89. Dolan had then taken charge at Rochdale, to whom City were eventually ordered to pay £40,000 because of the way in which Chetham had acquired his services in mid-season. Dolan brought Jeff Lee and Bernard Ellison from Rochdale with him to complete his management team, but they could not prevent City from going down.

Dolan and his No. 2 Lee tightened up the defence, but the goals dried up even though there was a 2-1 away win against champions-elect Oldham Athletic. City won only two of their remaining nine home games after the new management team had taken over and went down. At the end of the season the Tigers had won only five out of 19 games under Dolan – two of them

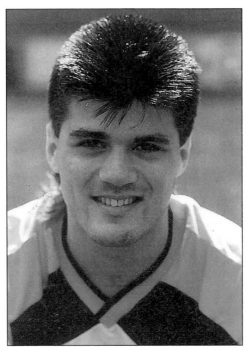

Hull City striker Andy Payton, whose 25 League goals were not enough to save them from relegation in 1990-91.

after relegation had been confirmed – and they were relegated on April 27, 1991, when they lost 1-0 at home to Brighton and Hove Albion. West Bromwich Albion accompanied them into the Third Division, but City finished three points adrift of them in bottom place and five points away from possible safety. The most perverse and remarkable statistic of such a moderate season, though, was that leading marksman Andy Payton scored 25 League goals in a relegated side, 18 of them coming while Ternent had still been in charge.

Things were slowly to go from bad to worse although I must confess that I may not be the best-qualified person to be objective about the 1995-96 season because the club chairman Martin Fish banned me from working as a journalist at Boothferry Park. But the stark facts and statistics can largely speak for themselves and they show that it was one of the worst in the club's history. Only the 1935-36 season can compare with it as the Tigers tumbled into the Third Division, by then the equivalent of the old Fourth Division, where they had previously spent just two seasons in their entire history.

As it was, it was impossible to paper over the cracks. The youth policy, which had for so long provided a solid base for the club's activities and even survival, had been eroded. Youngsters from the East Riding, for example, regularly slipped the net. By the end of the 1998-99 season players such as goalkeeper Paul Robinson and striker Richard Cresswell had played in the FA Premiership with Leeds United and Sheffield Wednesday respectively, while Lee Morris and Curtis Woodhouse had broken through into Sheffield United's first team. Even though the management team had been granted a much longer lifespan than many of their predecessors at Boothferry Park or their contemporaries elsewhere, the club lacked direction. It is true that money was tight, but Colin Appleton and Brian Horton had overcome that factor by producing promotion teams on comparatively small budgets in the 1980s with a combination of expertise, passion and organisation. And as had often been the case before, City found that a lack of progress eventually led to their downfall and heralded relegation.

After one win in their opening three League games, City crumbled and when they lost 3-2 at home to Shrewsbury Town on October 7, 1995, they went to the foot of the Second Division table – and stayed there for the remainder of the campaign. At that point the Tigers were in a run of 16 League games without a win, in which they took a mere seven points out of a possible 48. In addition, they sold forward Dean Windass, who had provided some encouraging moments in his second spell with the club after being released as a teenager in the days when their youth policy had been far more fruitful and the competition had been fiercer, to Aberdeen. Soon afterwards a 1-0 away win at York City with a late winner by Paul Fewings ended the barren sequence, but it merely led to another. Centre-back Rob Dewhurst broke his leg at Bournemouth a week after the success at York as eight more games failed to produce a win with a return of just three points out of a possible 24. In addition, City went 11 League games between August 26, 1995, and February 24, 1996, without a victory at Boothferry Park. A further six games without a win left any lingering hopes of an escape from relegation in tatters.

In the second half of the season young goalkeeper Roy Carroll established himself in the side and was later to follow in the footsteps of one of his recent predecessors, Alan Fettis, by becoming a full Northern Ireland international, but the season was dying on its feet and five games from the end of it relegation was confirmed after a 2-1 home defeat against Crewe Alexandra. The Tigers, who went through a lot of playing personnel in keeping with so many other relegation seasons, went on to lose their last five games and they finished a huge 21 points behind the sides who had only just stayed up. Furthermore, City were nine points behind Brighton and Hove Albion, the side immediately above them. And Terry Dolan had emulated Bob Brocklebank by becoming the second manager to take the Tigers down twice. To be fair to Brocklebank, though, he did at least take them up again in-between!

A further perverse statistic was that Dolan's immediate predecessor Stan Ternent was bypassing him on the way because he guided Bury to automatic promotion from the Third Division just as City were going down into it. Closer to home, however, trouble was brewing and it exploded into life in the Tigers' final game of the season. It was against Bradford City, who were striving for a place in the Play-offs, and it attracted a crowd of 8,965 to Boothferry Park, strangely the biggest home gate of the campaign. What naturally riled the loyal City fans, who were already at the end of their collective tether after events on the pitch, was that they were unceremoniously kicked out of their traditional South Stand haunt and ordered to watch the game from elsewhere. The switch was considered to be the ultimate snub and was arguably the worst public-relations exercise in the club's history. It hurried along the formation of a pressure group called Tigers 2000, who had had enough of the excuses and lack of achievement, wanted change for the better and decided to take on the stubborn powers-that-be who showed no signs of budging. It took them a little more than a confrontational year before their dreams came true.

The utter despair of the situation is that City are still in the Third Division as the century closes, they have shown few signs of escaping from it at the top end and they continue to go through the most depressing phase in their history. Fans have almost become immune to the broken promises and false dawns, but the disastrous 1995-96 season provided a relegation too far: no-one believes in miracles any more.

Chapter Nine

Near Misses

HULL City may have attained promotion only six times in their history, but there have been other occasions on which they have gone very close before it all ended in what might almost be considered the usual anti-climax. Luck has often seemed to desert the Tigers at crucial times when they might just have needed a rub of the green, but the consequences have normally been enlightening to say the least.

They have twice clinched promotion after just missing out, for example, but the first occasion that it happened to them, it left them a terrible legacy from which they have never recovered. There was initial optimism that City would soon join English soccer's elite after they had finished fifth in the Second Division in their first season in the Football League in 1905-06 even though they were still 18 points adrift of a promotion place. Three seasons later the Tigers finished fourth, but they were still seven points away from achieving their promotion objective.

In 1909-10, though, City had their first near miss with promotion and have spent the rest of the century cursing their ill-fortune from those formative years as a club. They failed to capitalise on the main prize in League terms when it was virtually in their grasp and have never been so tantalisingly close to achieving top-flight status since.

The Tigers were fortunate that goalscoring was not a problem that season because Jack Smith was as prolific as ever. He had been the Second Division's top marksman with 31 goals in 1907-08 and two years later he went one better to over-take his own club record. His 32 goals in just 35 League games in 1909-10 included four hat-tricks – against Lincoln City, close rivals Oldham Athletic, Stockport County and West Bromwich Albion in the penultimate match of the season as the promotion battle reached boiling-point. Jack Smith was well-supported by Arthur Temple with 16 League goals and Wallace Smith with 17. And both registered hat-tricks of their own – Temple in a 7-0 thrashing of Birmingham City and Wallace Smith against Clapton Orient.

But City leaked too many goals at times and it was a factor when the promotion race became so tight at the end of the season. There were only four realistic challengers for the two promotion spots because the others were reduced to also-rans. The Tigers were battling it out with Oldham, Manchester City and Derby County. And they had already lost 4-0 at Derby and 3-0 at Manchester City by the time that it all hinged on the final game of the season – at Oldham on April 30, 1910.

Generally, City had lasted the pace well throughout the season because they had opened it by taking 11 points out of a possible 12. They then had a sticky patch in which they won only two games out of ten before winning five out of the next six. A brief hiccup of three games without a win was followed by a spectacular sequence of 11 wins and one draw – at home to close rivals Derby – in 12 matches, culminating in a 5-1 mauling of mid-table West Bromwich Albion, in which Jack Smith recorded his final hat-trick of the season. Everything then depended on the last match of the campaign at Oldham.

City went into it two points clear of Athletic, who had not won any of their first five League games of the season, with little to choose between the two in terms of goal average, while Manchester City and Derby remained in contention. Oldham had developed a habit of securing vital victories because they had been the only side to defeat Manchester City twice and they had beaten Derby 4-0. By the time that the Tigers went to Oldham, Manchester City had all but clinched promotion, barring any spectacular adjustments to goal averages. The Tigers, meanwhile, still had a chance of winning the title and all that they needed to do at Oldham was to avoid defeat. A win or a draw would ensure promotion, but any defeat would be catastrophic because Oldham already had a superior goal average.

Athletic had been beaten only twice at home during the season and City were well aware that they were venturing into a decidedly testing environment. It was reported: "Oldham is not one of the most ideal places for a visiting team, especially when so much depends on the game. In addition to the players themselves being of a very robust nature – indeed, roughness is in the repertoire of some – the spectators are, to say the least, very partisan and, while applauding questionable tactics by their own men, are apt to resent even the most honest charge on the part of their opponents."

The Tigers were without left-back Jack McQuillan because of illness and injury and little went right for them. For a start, they did not like the condition of the pitch and it was reported: "The ground was in an absolutely abominable state. It was an indescribable puddle that was termed a ground. Whatever success Oldham have achieved has in no small measure been because of the difficulties that a visiting team have to meet with regard to the ground alone. From one end of the ground to the other, there is a slope of at least six feet, while across it there is a difference of between three and four feet."

City were behind after 18 minutes when the dangerous Tommy Broad scored and seven minutes later there was a mixture of irony and controversy. Alf Toward was thought to be well offside as he gave Oldham an important two-goal cushion – and what made it worse was the fact that he was an ex-Tiger. Ten minutes from time David Walders made it 3-0 to Oldham, who were promoted as runners-up to Manchester City, and the game ended amid various skirmishes, including one in which the Tigers' manager Ambrose Langley and chairman Alwyn Smith had to rescue Joe "Stanley" Smith from "some rough handling."

As it turned out, Oldham, City and Derby all finished on 53 points, one less than Manchester City. But Athletic had the best goal average of the trio – 2.03 – and the Tigers had to be content with third place on 1.74. City had missed out on promotion to the First Division in heart-breaking circumstances.

There was even a strange postscript to the season because it suddenly looked as if an opportunity might still present itself for City to be promoted to the First Division by the back door. It is hard to believe nowadays that Woolwich Arsenal, who had escaped relegation from the First Division by only two points, were in grave danger of folding in early part of the close season in 1910. Poor results and staff cuts "at the Arsenal works" had led to a big reduction in attendances and the club had already been reconstituted and re-formed during the season in an attempt to solve a major financial crisis. By the end of the season Arsenal desperately needed to raise a further £2,000 in £1 shares to reorganise the club and float them as a new company, but it was an ominous sign when chairman George Leavey resigned.

It was then strongly mooted that Arsenal might be taken over by Second Division Fulham. And if that had happened, it would almost certainly have meant that the new newly-merged club would take Fulham's place in the Second Division and there would be an extra vacancy in the First Division. The rules were generally interpreted as indicating that the Tigers would then "have a most decided right to a vacant position should there be one." But on May 18, 1910, the matter was resolved at a meeting between Arsenal and Fulham officials and a three-man delegation from the FA at London's Imperial Hotel. It emerged that Arsenal were to continue in their own right, three new directors were to be appointed and "under the arrangement all liabilities would be met if the club were adequately supported." In addition, the possibility of relocating the club would be reviewed in a year's time, but that was of no help to the Tigers' cause, of course. The First Division door had closed on them again and they have not yet opened it for the first time.

The following season City again finished fifth in the Second Division, but they were still seven points away from a promotion spot. They were well in contention by the end of 1910, but there must have been something in the 1911 water that upset them. They did not win a League game in January and February and then went nine matches without a victory before they ended their campaign with a 2-1 win at home to Lincoln City.

There was a similar kind of season in 1921-22 when City fell away in the second half of their programme. They had hauled themselves into the promotion pack by mid-December, beating Stoke City, who were to be promoted as the runners-up to Nottingham Forest at the end of the season, 7-1 at home along the way. But the Tigers did not win any of their five matches in February, drawing twice against close rivals West Ham United, and were then crucially beaten twice in the closing stages of the season by Barnsley, one of the other promotion candidates. City finished fifth again although they were just four points away from a promotion place this time.

In the 1930s City had their highs and lows – their only excursion to the FA Cup semi-finals at the start of the decade and their first-ever promotion campaign, which were offset by two relegation seasons. But they were almost back in the Second Division by the day war broke out because they went frustratingly close to promotion in 1937-38.

Ian Butler above the old Hull City railway engine nameplate at Boothferry Park after joining the club in January 1965.

City found a goalscoring partnership for the second time in the decade. In 1932-33 they had the Third Division North title on the strength of goals supplied by Bill McNaughton and Russell Wainscoat. Five years later John MacNeill and Jack Fryer were both on the mark 23 times in the League campaign. MacNeill hit an early-season hat-trick against Barrow and then had an autumn run of eight goals in eight games, scoring in all but one of them. City lost only four League games up to mid-January in 1938, after which MacNeill became gradually less prolific. John Pears scored the club's only other hat-trick that season in a 10-0 trouncing of Southport at Anlaby Road, but Fryer was a consistent marksman throughout what was his only season with the club, six times scoring twice in the League.

In the second half of the season the Tigers had a run in which they took just one point out of a possible eight, but then they put together a sequence of eight games without defeat to remain on the promotion trail. A 2-1 defeat at Southport was followed by a run of five games without defeat in which City did the double over York City in a three-day period. On April 22, 1933, the Tigers had won 2-1 at York on their way to promotion: on April 23, 1938, coincidentally, Fryer's 17th-minute goal gave them a 1-0 win at York and the omens for another promotion season then looked good. On May 1, 1933, City had beaten York 2-1 at home on their way to promotion: on April 25, 1938, equally coincidentally, they defeated York 3-1 at home in the return game, so the omens for another promotion season still looked good.

But the Tigers had one more major obstacle to overcome – a home game against Tranmere Rovers, who represented the biggest threat to their aspirations other than

Doncaster Rovers in what had become a tight promotion race. The vital clash actually took place on FA Cup Final day when Preston North End beat Huddersfield Town with a penalty in the last minute of extra time. But there had also been plenty of drama at Anlaby Road because Rovers became the first side to do the double over City that season when a shot by William Eden struck the underside of the bar and flew into the net for the only goal of the game. Yet in the second half MacNeill hit the bar for the Tigers and the ball ricocheted to safety.

An equaliser then would not have been enough to ensure promotion for City, but it put Tranmere in a near-impregnable position because of Doncaster's inferior goal average. And the Tigers' final game of the season – their third successive one at home – ended in anti-climax because they could only draw 1-1 with Crewe Alexandra. Significantly, it was the Tigers' eighth draw of the season at Anlaby Road, six of them coming in the second half of the season as they threw away vital promotion points. In the end only six points separated the top six and City finished third, one point behind Doncaster and three behind Tranmere. The clash with Crewe, furthermore, was a second benefit match for goalkeeper George Maddison, then the longest-serving player in the club's history. He did not play in it and he was released at the end of the season after 14 years with the club: City instead retained a youngster who had not yet played in the first team, a goalkeeper called Billy Bly who would stay with the Tigers for much longer. Like Maddison, he was to bounce back after injury time after time. The collective pain for City then, however, was the disappointment of missing out on promotion.

After their relegation to the Third Division in 1959-60, City made steady progress as they finished 11th, 10th, 10th and eighth. But manager Cliff Britton was coming under increasing pressure to spend the money so graciously provided by

Hull City in 1964-65 before Ken Wagstaff, Ian Butler and Ken Houghton had been signed for a total of £120,000. Back row (left to right): Gerry Summers, Brian Garvey, Norman Corner, Mike Williams, Maurice Swan, Mick Milner, Les Collinson, George Cummins; middle row, Paul Feasey, Chris Chilton, Andy Davidson, Chris Simpkin, Mick Brown, Alan Jarvis, Terry Heath; front row, Doug Clarke, Dennis Butler, Len Sharpe, Ray Henderson, Eric McMillan, Billy Wilkinson, Ron Young, John McSeveney.

chairman Harold Needler for team strengthening and ground improvements at Boothferry Park. The cash injection came from Needler's gift to the club of £200,000 worth of shares in his Hoveringham Gravel business concern early in 1963: their value soon increased to £500,000 and Britton invested in some new players, such as Dennis Butler, Ron "Chips" Rafferty and Terry Heath. But he had been frugal and it soon became clear as the 1964-65 season unfolded that a little extra input into the playing side would be needed.

The first 11 League games produced just three wins and Chris Chilton was unsettled. He was briefly replaced at centre-forward by Norman Corner and Ron Rafferty before he returned for a home game against Barnsley, the first under the club's new, improved floodlighting system with six pylons, on October 3, 1964. Only four pylons were working for that opening match, but it did not deter the Tigers, who won 7-0. The transfer-listed Chilton returned to score four goals, the first coming after just 12 seconds when it was laid on by teenage winger Ron Young with his first touch in League soccer, and Ray Henderson chipped in with a hat-trick. Two more home wins followed against Carlisle United and Reading in less than a week. All six pylons were by now working and City's form was as bright as they were. They next won 3-1 at Luton Town and went on a seven-match undefeated run. But when it ended with successive defeats against Grimsby Town and Peterborough United, manager Cliff Britton acted decisively.

He signed inside-forward Ken Wagstaff from Mansfield Town, where his formative years had largely been governed by former City hero Raich Carter. The fee was £40,000, high in those days in general and also a club record. Wagstaff scored on his debut in a 3-1 home win over Exeter City on November 21, 1964, and Chris Chilton had a deadly goalscoring partner to take some of the weight off his broad shoulders. After a 2-1 away defeat against Oldham Athletic, the Tigers went on a 14-match unbeaten run. It was to include sequences of five wins and then four wins with only a draw between them, but Britton's spending spree had not ended.

He had been linked with a move for Rotherham United's inside-forward Albert Bennett and in the first week of 1965 he twice raided Millmoor. But he did not take Bennett: instead he ushered in the New Year in by signing left-winger Ian Butler and the following week he snapped up his inside-forward partner Ken Houghton. Both

Les Collinson heads home for Hull City in a 3-1 home win over Exeter City on Ken Wagstaff's debut for the club in November 1964.

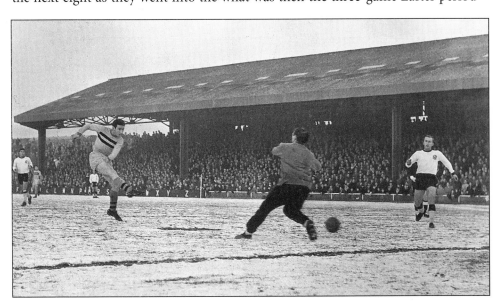

cost £40,000 and City could not stop scoring goals as they emerged as strong promotion candidates, finishing off January with a 3-2 home win over one of the pacesetters, Bristol Rovers, in front of 28,399 fans, the highest attendance of the season.

The long-serving Doug Clarke made way for Butler as John McSeveney swapped wings, while Ray Henderson was temporarily out of favour as Houghton took his place. It was curious that Clarke's absence meant that City had lost a player with one of the fiercest shots around, but they had brought in Houghton, who could strike a ball with just as much ferocity.

City had only one win in four games in March, but they took seven points from the next eight as they went into the what was then the three-game Easter period –

Hull City's John McSeveney heads past Reading's goalkeeper Arthur Wilkie and defender Maurice Evans for the only goal of the match at Boothferry Park in October 1964.

Hull City's Ray Henderson shoots past Port Vale's goalkeeper Reg Davies in a 4-0 home win in December 1964.

something which might be too tough for some of today's over-paid, mollycoddled professionals. It was to bring them just one point out of six and the promotion opportunity had all but gone. They faced a trip to close rivals Mansfield Town, but lost 2-1: they met Southend United twice, losing 2-1 at Roots Hall and then drawing 0-0 in the return encounter on Easter Monday.

The ironic touches continued. Wagstaff missed some good chances in his first game against Mansfield since he had left them, as goalkeeper Colin Treharne defied the Tigers with an inordinate amount of luck. Wagstaff did score City's goal, but it came with a header – ironically, his first-ever for anyone at Field Mill. Southend, meanwhile, had become City's bogey side that season. They had knocked them out of the Football League Cup, winning 3-1 at Roots Hall after a goalless draw at Boothferry Park and they became stumbling-blocks in the League. In the goalless draw at Boothferry Park that ended the Easter programme, their goalkeeper Ian McKechnie repeatedly denied City. The following summer – after the Tigers had won promotion – McKechnie was to join the Tigers himself when cover was urgently needed for Maurice Swan.

The Easter disaster left City in third place in the table with one game left. Carlisle United and Mansfield were above them and had to meet one another: Gillingham, Brentford and Bristol City had fewer games and were breathing down the Tigers' necks. City beat Brentford 2-1 at home in their final game, but it was not enough: Carlisle went up as champions on 60 points, Bristol City pipped Mansfield

Hull City in 1969-70. Back row (left to right): Dennis Butler, Don Beardsley, Frank Banks, Ian McKechnie, Paddy Greenwood, Tom Wilson, Ray Pettit, John McSeveney (coach); front row, Alan Jarvis, Ken Houghton, Ken Wagstaff, Chris Chilton, Billy Wilkinson, Ian Butler, Chris Simpkin.

for the second promotion spot as they both finished on 59 and City ended up in fourth spot on 58. It had been a devastating finale to City's season after it had gained so much momentum bit by bit.

When former Northern Ireland and Arsenal centre-half Terry Neill took over as City's player-manager in the summer of 1970, he inherited a strong squad from his predecessor Cliff Britton, who had been moved to a role as general manager. The basis of the formidable forward-line of Chris Chilton, Ken Wagstaff, Ken Houghton and Ian Butler were in situ for the last time and Stuart Pearson, a future England international, was breaking through into the first team. City remained in promotion contention for most of the season, but the goals uncharacteristically dried up from mid-January onwards and yet another season was to end in anti-climax. It was typified by a week in early March when the Tigers lost 1-0 at home to Oxford United a few days after vitally winning 2-1 against promotion rivals Sheffield United in the infamous Battle of Bramall Lane in which players from both sides were called together and ordered to calm down. But bit by bit the First Division dream was once more about to fade and die and City finished fifth, five points behind the Blades, who were the runners-up to Leicester City.

It is often thought that promoted clubs begin the following season on a high with the same buoyancy, spirit and togetherness providing a knock-on effect. And that is precisely what happened after City had gone up from the Fourth Division in 1982-83. They did not lose any of their opening 11 League games under Colin Appleton's management the following season and the sequence included some impressive home wins – 4-1 over Burnley, 5-0 over Millwall, then managed by George Graham, and 4-1 over Sheffield United. And the Tigers did not lose an away game until a 2-1 defeat at Exeter City in early December, but even then that setback was followed by four League wins in a row up to the end of 1983. The omens were promising for City to be promoted in two successive seasons for the first time ever.

Former England goalkeeper Peter Shilton let in a lot of goals against Hull City in his time. This time Chris Chilton beats him in a 3-0 home win over Leicester City in December 1970.

Chris Chilton scores the first goal of his last hat-trick for Hull City in a 4-0 victory over Sunderland at Boothferry Park in January 1971.

The Tigers did not win their only two League games in January 1984 and at the end of February they lost two consecutive Third Division matches for the only time that season, but they were still in the leading pack. And they put together another run of four wins in a row, which included starting April with an emphatic 4-1 success at close rivals Wimbledon. But suddenly City's away form deserted them and they lost at Scunthorpe United, Orient and Port Vale in succession. It was all the more galling that Scunthorpe and Port Vale were to be relegated only a season after having been promoted with the Tigers. A goalless draw at home to Bristol Rovers, who had only just slipped out of the promotion stakes themselves, heightened the tension.

Oxford United, managed by Appleton's fellow Yorkshireman and old friend Jim Smith, and Wimbledon, who had also gone up with City a year earlier, had already made sure of promotion. It was left to the Tigers and Sheffield United to battle it out for the third promotion place. City had one game left – against Burnley at Turf Moor. And that made it all the more dramatic because the Tigers had controversially failed to get to Burnley for the game because of adverse weather conditions on the M62 four months earlier. City had defeated Burnley by a three-goal margin on the opening day of the season: now they had to beat them by three goals or more in the last game to go up.

Sheffield United had finished their programme with 83 points from 46 games and a goal difference of 33. City went to Burnley with 80 points from 45 games and a goal difference of 31. If the goal differences at the end of the 90 minutes at Turf Moor were the same, then the Blades would go up by dint of having scored more goals during the season. As it was, both sides finished with a goal difference of 33 because the Tigers won 2-0 with goals by Brian Marwood. United had scored a total of 86 goals compared with City's tally of 71 and duly went into the Second Division.

And if that were not sensational enough, Colin Appleton resigned as City's manager immediately after the match to take charge of Swansea City. Who needs the Play-offs nowadays to provide end-of-season drama? Skipper Garreth Roberts summed the feelings of the devastated players when he recalled: "It was probably the most emotional game I've ever played in because the situation gripped the whole city. The support we had at the game was unbelievable and to say that we were disappointed by the outcome is the biggest understatement imaginable. The feeling in the dressing-room after the match was awful. Everyone was so quiet and hardly anyone spoke for a long time. Some players just wandered off to find their own little space, collect their own thoughts and try to put it all into perspective. About 15 minutes after the game another bombshell hit us when Colin said he was resigning as manager. He said he had had enough and even if we'd gone up, I think he would have resigned in any case for whatever reasons. There were repeated attempts by players to make him change his mind, but he was adamant about his decision."

Brian Marwood had scored the two goals at Burnley that had given City the chance of defying the odds that night, but neither could he underestimate the

The long-serving Garreth Roberts, who led Hull City to two promotions.

intense emotions of it all. He reflected: "That night at Burnley will stand out in my mind for the rest of my life. You could not have stage-managed a better situation. There was a tremendous following from Hull, some fans from Sheffield United and a little bit of needle from the time when the match had been postponed. It was an ideal situation for a cliff-hanger. We scored in the first half, hit the post, missed a couple of good chances and kept battling away to get a second, but, strangely enough, we didn't play very well after that and the last 15 minutes were a total anti-climax. At the end I remember crying on the pitch, as did some of the other lads. Emotionally, it had taken everything out of me. I remember thinking afterwards that the whole thing was strange. We were so numb and down after the match and, when we heard about Colin, everybody was upset. Everybody just went quiet although a few of the lads then tried to talk him out of it. Unfortunately Colin never got the recognition he deserved. It looked bad that night – almost as if he were leaving a sinking ship – but he was a man of high principles."

It was, in fact, Marwood's last match for City because he joined Sheffield Wednesday in a £115,000 deal during that summer of 1984 and later made a brief appearance as a substitute for England during his Arsenal days. And he added: "To be fair, the move came as a great pick-me-up. It cheered me up because that match at Burnley had stayed at the back of my mind." But when the Tigers lost 1-0 at home to eventual champions Oxford United that season, Marwood had a penalty saved by goalkeeper Steve Hardwick. If he had scored from the spot, City would have been promoted. If other bits of luck had gone City's way on other occasions, they would doubtless have gone up. It all serves to show that the dividing-line between success and failure is minute at times.

Brian Marwood, who gained England honours after leaving Hull City.

Nowadays, though, it is basically impossible to miss out on promotion in the same dramatic circumstances. If a team do not go up automatically, then they have another bite of the cherry with three others in the end-of-season Play-offs. They create extra interest and bring in extra money: there is also the added opportunity of a Play-off Final trip to Wembley. Yet they are hardly fair. A side who have just been pipped for automatic promotion can go into the Play-offs with their morale low after missing out: conversely, a side can have only a slightly above-average season until putting a good run together in the later stages to reach the Play-offs and go into them on a high. Accordingly, a side might end up gaining promotion at the expense of one who has done far better over the course of a season. And Hull City can always look back and quote a few examples of the end-of-season dramas that have been every bit as acute and heart-breaking as anything produced by the Play-offs system.

Chapter Ten

Tight Corners

I F HULL City have had their frustrating moments of just missing out on promotion, then there have been other seasons when they have been eternally grateful for narrowly avoiding relegation at the other end of the soccer scale. It is often a football trend that if a side end in mid-table respectability in any division season after season, then the odds seem to favour relegation rather than promotion sooner or later. It may well be that clubs lose a sense of ambition, momentum and drive in such circumstances and things go from not so bad to a lot worse before it really hits them.

It is always difficult to be definitive as to how tight any corner might be, of course. For example, a side may be struggling for most of the season, gradually haul themselves up by their bootlaces after digging deep into their mental resources and not only avoid relegation but also reach the fringes of mid-table respectability. On other occasions a side might think that they are in mid-table security, lose their drive, method and, most significantly, their professionalism and suddenly find themselves in the proverbial mire before they know it. Often that can result in relegation for the simple reason that teams in that predicament tend to panic because they are new to the crisis just when time to running out for them. If they are lucky, teams might just get out of their tight corner after giving themselves the biggest fright of their footballing lives.

In the early days City seemed to maintain an equilibrium and there was greater hopes of making progress into the First Division rather than going down. For many years their worst season in the Second Division came in 1923-24 when they finished 17th after becoming draw specialists – 17 of them in 42 games, in fact. They drew their first four League games – against Leicester City and Clapton Orient twice – and generally struggled to score goals, but their goal average was good because they did not concede too many, either. They won only two of their first 16 League outings, but manager Bill McCracken, who was in his first full season in charge, wrested control of team matters from the club's selection committee, everything

Raich Carter goes out to face Doncaster Rovers on his comeback as a Hull City player in December 1951.

ticked over nicely after that and City were rarely in any danger of relegation. In the end they finished four points clear of Nelson, who went down with the bottom club, Bristol City.

The Tigers did achieve the real thing twice – relegation in 1929-30 and 1935-36 – but it was not as if they were forever in danger. It was in the 1950s, though, that they more or less turned flirting with relegation into an art form for a spell. They never fully capitalised on the passion and high expectations created by the early

seasons of the Raich Carter era and regularly found them looking precariously over their shoulders in the old Second Division. For three seasons out for four, they diced with relegation death, but escaped. It did them little good, though, because they finally went down in 1955-56.

The slippery slope began in 1951-52. City made an inconsistent start to the season and then the fans were shocked to find out that the unthinkable had happened – their great hero Raich Carter had resigned in September 1951. Midway through the month they embarked on a run of 12 games without a win – ten defeats and two draws – that plunged them into trouble. The Tigers tried unsuccessfully to persuade Jack Crayston, who later took charge of Arsenal, to take over as manager, so they ended up operating without one and it was not until a decision was taken to hold Carter to the playing side of his contract that something approaching normality was restored. Carter returned to the side on December 8, 1951, and the barren spell was immediately over as City beat Doncaster Rovers 2-0 at Boothferry Park.

The prolific Syd Gerrie hit 24 goals in a struggling side that season, including four in a 5-0 home win over Bury, but the Tigers' away form continued to cause concern. In the last two months of the season they lost 6-0 at Sheffield Wednesday, 5-0 at Everton and 4-0 at Nottingham Forest, so there could be no room for complacency. The Good Friday thrashing at Everton, for example, brought eight changes for the visit to Forest the next day, but Viggo Jensen was controversially sent off and the outcome was another serious setback. But on Easter Monday City earned themselves some respite in front of a 30,240 crowd at Boothferry Park when Gerrie returned after a knee injury and scored the only goal of the second meeting with Everton from 39-year-old Eddie Burbanks' free-kick seven minutes from time.

Gerrie pulled a muscle, though, and it forced him to miss the last home game of the season. It was against mid-table Brentford and was acknowledged as Carter's last appearance at Boothferry Park before his retirement. City had not lost at home since late November and their form at Boothferry Park again stood them in good stead as they hammered the Bees 4-1. But the attention then reverted to their poor away form for the final game of the season against Doncaster Rovers at the Belle Vue Ground. The Tigers needed a point to be certain to staying up, but their only away win had been back in September 1950 when they had defeated struggling Coventry City 4-1. As it turned out, Coventry and Queen's Park Rangers were relegated and City would have stayed up even if they had lost at Doncaster. But they ended their away jinx by fittingly winning 1-0 with the goal coming 12 minutes from the end from Carter on his last appearance for the club. They had to play for an hour with ten men after the injury-prone Garrie had damaged his shoulder, but the Tigers finished three points clear of the bottom two in 18th place.

Even though the memorable Raich Carter era was over, little changed for City in 1952-53 because they again finished three points clear of a relegation spot in 18th position. Bob Jackson, whose trademark was a bow-tie, had succeeded Carter as manager, but Syd Gerrie was again the leading goalscorer and he was given adequate support from Ken Horton and Viggo Jensen.

But a promising start to the season was eroded by a run of seven successive defeats up to the end of November. City's fortunes picked up a little, but the dawn of 1953 presented more problems when they failed to win any of their six League games in January and February. They began March with three wins in a row, but the situation was tense. Barnsley were rooted to the bottom of the table even though they had beaten the Tigers 5-1 earlier in the season, but it remained to be seen as to who would go down with them. City took three points out of six during Easter, but then lost 2-1 to a late winner at fellow strugglers Bury.

The Tigers picked up another point in a 1-1 draw at home to Leicester City, but then came another crunch encounter against fellow strugglers in the last game of the season at Boothferry Park. The opposition were Southampton and victory would ensure that City avoided the drop, but they had injury worries about forwards Fionan "Paddy" Fagan, Ken Harrison, Brian Cripsey and Eddie Burbanks, all of whom were ruled out. As a result, 19-year-old Brian Bulless was given his League debut on the left-wing and he achieved instant hero status. City won 1-0 and Bulless scored with the winner with his trusty left foot from Johnny Linaker's 51st-minute corner. The Tigers then lost 2-0 away to Notts County, another of the struggling sides, but Southampton went down with Barnsley, who finished 15 points adrift. City ended their programme by showing off the unpredictable side of their nature – something which has, of course, driven the fans to distraction for so long – by winning 2-0 at Second Division champions Sheffield United with goals by Syd Gerrie and Jimmy Duthie and finishing three points clear of the Saints.

In 1953-54 City improved a little to finish 15th in the Second Division, but the following season their contrary nature resurfaced. The initial omens were promising because they won four consecutive games after losing 2-0 at home to Leeds United on the opening day of the season. The Tigers were beaten only three times in their first 13 matches, but they failed to win any of their ten League games in

November, December and January. And after a 2-1 success at Middlesbrough, they won only once in their next ten outings. The danger signs were there and they cost manager Bob Jackson his job.

On March 17, 1955, City's board announced that Jackson had been given "leave of absence" even though he was under contract to the club until the end of June 1957. He appeared in his office as usual, insisting: "I am just cleaning up my affairs and having a comfortable smoke." The directors, meanwhile, announced the appointment of Bob Brocklebank, who had been scouting for West Bromwich Albion, as Jackson's successor. And "Gentleman Bob," as he was known, agreed to work without a contract. Jackson, in the meantime, was contemplating possible legal action for an alleged breach of contract.

One of Brocklebank's first tasks was to sell two of City's forwards, Ken Harrison and Alf Ackerman, to Derby County for a total of £8,000. It was a bold step for one

Bob Jackson, who was controversially given "leave of absence" as Hull City's manager in March 1955.

Bob Crosbie (left) and Alf Ackerman, whose goals saved Hull City in 1954-55.

simple reason – the Tigers' problems had been caused by a general dearth of goals and Ackerman and Bob Crosbie, who had scored all four in a 4-2 home win over Ipswich Town in the early part of the season, had been responsible for most of them. They ended up with 11 apiece that season out of an overall tally of 44, which was the joint lowest anywhere in the Football League with Chester, who propped up the Third Division North table. Even former England international Wilf Mannion, brought out of retirement at the end of 1954, scored just once.

There were successive 4-1 defeats against Bury and Blackburn Rovers before Syd Gerrie scored both winners in consecutive 1-0 victories over Bury and Fulham. The return game with the Shakers at the end of the Easter programme was noteworthy because it marked the only League appearance for City by goalkeeper Ron Capewell, who kept a clean sheet in it. The Tigers had by then ensured their survival, but they failed to win any of their final four games and that run included defeats at Ipswich Town and Derby County, the two sides who were relegated. They provided timely warnings even though City still escaped the drop by six points after finishing 19th, but they went unheeded because they were relegated the following season.

The Tigers next walked a relegation tightrope in the old Third Division in 1979-80 and it was only in their penultimate League game of the 46 that they escaped. Hopes had been high at the start of the season because City had finished eighth under Ken Houghton's management in their first season back in the Third Division. But their form was inconsistent until mid-October, after which it went from bad to

Bob Brocklebank (right) with secretary Cyril Lee on his first day as Hull City's manager in March 1955.

worse. The Tigers were knocked out of the FA Cup in the first round by Carlisle United and went 13 League games without a win. After the ninth game in the sequence – a 7-2 defeat at Brentford – Houghton was sacked in December 1979. Coach Wilf McGuinness, the former England international who went on to become a popular after-dinner speaker and to help out with match-day hospitality at his old club Manchester United, and the long-serving Andy Davidson, were also shown the door.

City hero Chris Chilton survived to take over briefly as caretaker manager, but the long-term replacements were Mike Smith, who had been national team manger of Wales, coach Cyril Lea, who was working with his old Ipswich Town colleague Brian Talbot for top Football Conference side Rushden and Diamonds by 1999, and youth development officer Bobby Brown.

Smith, untried in League management, took over at the start of 1980 and made changes, but he could not wave a football magic wand. Striker Trevor Phillips, the club's joint record signing when he moved from Rotherham United for £75,000 the previous summer, left for Chester City and defender Peter Skipper was loaned to

Hull City in 1971-72. Back row (left to right): back row, Ken Knighton, Ken Houghton, Frank Banks, Roger de Vries, Stuart Blampey, Paul O'Riley; middle row, Ian Butler, Paddy Greenwood, Don Beardsley, Ian McKechnie, Peter Walters, Ray Pettit, Chris Simpkin, Tommy Docherty (assistant manager); front row, Stuart Pearson, Ken Wagstaff, Terry Neill (player-manager), Malcolm Lord, Billy Wilkinson.

Scunthorpe United and then went to Darlington. Brian Marwood, who was to go on and play briefly for England, was given occasional opportunities and in came goalkeeper Tony Norman, who was to prove to be a bargain signing when he cost £30,000 from Burnley, centre-back Dale Roberts from Ipswich Town, where he has latterly been on the coaching staff, and Welsh international striker Nick Deacy, who had played in Belgium and Holland for most of his career and cost a club record £95,000 from Vitesse Arnhem.

Keith Edwards continued to score some vital goals, but the Tigers' form remained inconsistent and they remained in grave danger of going into the Fourth Division for the first time in their history. A 2-1 home win over Brentford towards the end of April provided a lifeline, but a lot depended on the penultimate game of the season at Boothferry Park. It was watched by just 3,297 fans, but that was an achievement in itself even though it was only marginally higher than what was then the lowest League attendance in the club's history – 3,235 against Newport County in April 1962. Most of the rest of Hull's sporting public had, after all, gone to Wembley that day to watch the Rugby League Challenge Cup Final between Hull FC and Hull Kingston Rovers. But Edwards scored the only goal of the game at Boothferry Park that afternoon, City survived and the players waved to the faithful few from the directors' box afterwards even though they were celebrating avoiding failure rather than being successful. The Tigers lost 1-0 at home to Bury in their final game, but were able to give League debuts to Ian Bennyworth, his only senior

appearance, and Steve McClaren, Manchester United's assistant manager when they completed their celebrated 1999 treble.

It was only temporary respite because City were relegated to the Fourth Division after finishing bottom the following season and by the latter half of the 1981-82 season their plight was desperate, especially in terms of finance. Towards the end of February 1982 chairman Christopher Needler put the club into receivership and that led to the sackings of Mike Smith and Cyril Lea. Chris Chilton and Bobby Brown were made joint caretaker managers as City battled for survival – not against relegation this time, but as a club as a whole. Les Mutrie, more recently a publican in his native North-East, scored in nine successive League games – 14 goals in total in the sequence, including four against Hartlepool United – and the Tigers won 12 games out of 21 in receivership as the players fought for their footballing lives – both collectively and individually. At the end of the season Don Robinson took over the reins as chairman and the Tigers had survived a close shave of a different kind. They lived to fight another day as a club after getting out of the tightest of their financially tight corners.

Relegation was never really a serious threat from the Second Division in 1998-99 even though City finished 21st, just one place clear of the drop. The Tigers had a five-point cushion over Shrewsbury Town, who went down with Birmingham City and Walsall. Leeds United legend Eddie Gray, one of soccer's genuine nice guys, had been appointed manager in the summer, but there was a general inconsistency even though Keith Edwards scored 26 League goals. Matters improved after a mid-season trip to Bermuda, from which the City party flew home on the same evening as the Lockerbie air tragedy, and there was only one defeat in seven League games and an

Hull City in 1981-82, when their plight seemed desperate. Back row (left to right): Steve Hoolickin, Bobby McNeil, Brian Ferguson, Billy Whitehurst, Les Mutrie, Stuart Eccleston; middle row, Chris Chilton (reserve coach), Dale Roberts, Nick Deacy, Tony Norman, Bobby Brown (youth development officer), John Davies, Steve Richards, Craig Norrie, Jeff Radcliffe (physiotherapist); seated, Keith Edwards, Dave Kynman, Steve McClaren, Brian Marwood, Micky Horswill, Mike Smith (manager), Cyril Lea (assistant manager), Garreth Roberts, Dennis Booth, Paul Moss, Gary Swann; front row, Andy Hurst, Mike Gray, Ian Davis, Andy Flounders, Mike Davies.

FA Cup run that produced a capacity 20,058 crowd for a fifth-round tie at home to Liverpool. City led 2-1 at halftime, but lost 3-2 and the rot set in. They had an FA Cup hangover and lost their next six League games. Furthermore, they won only once in their last 18 League matches as the bottom fell out of their season. The Tigers had never been in serious trouble, but it was enough for Gray and his assistant Dennis Booth to be fired after just one season as a management team.

In 1989-90 City had one of those seasons in which they started particularly badly, but rallied bit by bit so that they finished in an acceptable mid-table placing that had looked most unlikely amid the initial doom and gloom. Colin Appleton had started his second spell in charge at Boothferry Park and the Tigers were in a tight corner when they failed to win any of their opening 16 League games. They lost six and drew ten before winning 3-2 away to Bradford City thanks to a last-minute goal by Ian McParland in Stan Ternent's first match in charge as manager after Appleton's reign had been dramatically brief this time. The dreadful opening left City as candidates for relegation to the Fourth Division again, but their revival

Les Mutrie, who had a prolific goalscoring run for Hull City in 1981-82.

under Ternent's management was so impressive that they finished 14th in the table. It included a run of four wins out of four during the festive period, during which Andy Payton scored the first Football League goal anywhere in the 1990s in a 3-2 success over Sunderland after an early start at Boothferry Park on New Year's Day. They still had their worrying moments until a late run of six wins and one draw in seven games left everyone to wonder what the fuss had really been all about.

The 1992-93 season, in contrast, worked the other way and was more akin to 1988-89. City had gone down from the old Second Division in 1990-91 and two years later they were nearly relegated from the new Second Division. There had been an optimistic start to the season under manager Terry Dolan with four wins and a draw from the first five games, but then the Tigers plunged down the table when they took only three points from draws out of a possible 36 from their next 12 matches. There was only one defeat in the next eight League outings, but City were generally struggling to score goals and they became entrenched in the lower half of the division. They were never realistic relegation candidates, but they lost their final four games and descended to 20th in the table, their lowest placing of the season. The Tigers finished three points clear of Preston North End, who were in the first relegation position, and they were probably relieved that the season finished when it did.

Yet towards the end of the 20th century City's fortunes were at their lowest ebb ever. Between 1996 and 1999 they had the three worst seasons ever in their history in what was by then the Third Division and their status as a League club was thrown more and more into question.

In 1996-97 the Tigers finished 17th in the Third Division and set two unwanted attendance records for home games. They were watched by a crowd of just 1,775

Hull City at the start of 1989-90. Back row (left to right): Mike Smith, Les Thompson, Malcolm Murray, Leigh Jenkinson, Paul Waites, Andy Payton, Paul Mudd; middle row, Tom Wilson (assistant manager), Jeff Radcliffe (physiotherapist), Nicky Brown, Peter Swan, David Cleminshaw, Billy Whitehurst, Iain Hesford, Steve Terry, Gavin Kelly, Richard Jobson, Neil Buckley, Dale Roberts (youth coach); front row, Ian McParland, Wayne Jacobs, Ken de Mange, Billy Askew, Don Robinson (chairman), Colin Appleton (manager), Coun. Terry Geraghty, Garreth Roberts, Lee Warren, Keith Edwards, Mark Calvert.

when they beat Torquay United on November 20, 1996: it was their lowest-ever League attendance. And only 553 hardy souls turned up at Boothferry Park to watch them defeat Chester City 3-1 in the Auto Windscreens Shield: it was the lowest attendance ever in any accepted competitive match. The Tigers, accordingly, remained in a tight corner financially. Chairman Martin Fish and his fellow directors Christopher Needler and Richard Chetham were cornered. The management team of Terry Dolan, Jeff Lee and Bernard Ellison, who had been installed towards the end of January 1991, were also cornered. The pressure group Tigers 2000 turned up the heat on the unpopular regime and something had to give: it did and just before the start of the 1997-98 campaign they were all replaced.

Tennis supremo David Lloyd and former Hull FC rugby-league player Tim Wilby assumed command in a takeover and former England striker Mark Hateley was installed as player-manager. They inherited a club in total disarray and they needed to buy time. As it was, they could not work miracles, the new dawn was fraught by misunderstandings, miscalculations and mistrust and a great opportunity was squandered. The team turned the concept of away defeats into their speciality – there were 20 out of 23. Only a 1-0 win at Cambridge United with a goal by Mark Greaves and two 2-2 draws at Hartlepool United and Brighton and Hove Albion spared City from the ultimate travelling humiliation. They did a little better at home and scored reasonably regularly, including a 7-4 victory over Swansea City that set a new aggregate goals record for a game at Boothferry Park. But the Tigers managed just 41 points – six fewer than the amount with which Hereford United had gone out of the League a year earlier – and finished in their lowest-ever position – 90th out of 92. Brighton were six points behind them, but they were both under remarkably little pressure thanks to the tale of Doncaster Rovers' footballing torment and tragedy. Rovers won only four games and finished on 20 points to drop out of the League. It was significant, though, that their last League victory was at home to the Tigers on April 4, 1998, when Adie MIke scored the only goal of the match in the last minute. There but for fortune…

There was an improvement of one place in 1998-99 when City finished 21st. But it was more of a near miss than the previous season because the equivalent of Doncaster Rovers did not emerge and relegation from the Football League was not to be decided until the final minute of the final day at Carlisle when on-loan goalkeeper Jimmy Glass saved them with a goal that sent Scarborough down in their place. The Tigers lost 2-0 away to Swansea City and were able to contemplate comfortably on what might have been, but they still finished only five points clear of Scarborough, who went out of the League.

The public, though, were thankful for that small mercy because City had been six points adrift – apparently without a paddle, too – at the bottom of the 92 League clubs at one stage. As the last year of the 20th century dawned, they had won only four Third Division games out of 24: the loyal fans, accustomed to being let down so often, had probably been hoping to be given maps of England as their main Christmas presents because there was every sign that they would need to know the way to some new destinations in the realms of non-League soccer in 1999-2000. City fans probably did not let in the New Year: instead they arguably wished that it would go away and never happen because of a clerical error!

Hull City's player-manager, Warren Joyce.

The prospects were bleak, but there had been a lot of changes although it still remained to be seen whether they were for the better and a rescue act was urgently required. Luckily, the club's paddle was restored and they found a new chairman and management team to steer the Tigers to safety.

Tom Belton took over chairman from David Lloyd, who retained the ownership of Boothferry Park itself, and he was backed by a group of businessmen who in general seemed to have had strong links with Sheffield United in the past. Belton, previously Scunthorpe United's chairman, had longed to get back into League soccer: more appropriately, he was the first media-friendly chairman since the halcyon days of Don Robinson. He soon ended Mark Hateley's unhappy reign as manager, giving the job on a caretaker basis to midfield player Warren Joyce, who had been helping out on the backroom staff after coach Billy Kirkwood had returned to his native Scotland with St. Johnstone. Hateley departed early in November 1998, but initially things did not really improve much at all, so it came as a source of some concern when Belton opted to give the untried Joyce the manager's job until the end of the season. Joyce brought in former Nottingham Forest captain John McGovern, whom he had known from their days together at Bolton Wanderers, and gradually they worked a miracle. They were lucky that they were permitted the financial scope to bring in several new players, but they built a base by making the team solid and hard to beat. They lost only four of their final 22 League games from the advent of 1999: equally crucially, they had won ten and remembered how to pick up points on a regular basis on their travels.

The Tigers had hauled themselves back from the precipice of Football League anonymity and the fact that they were the second-best supported team in the Third Division behind promoted Cardiff City was a lasting testimony to the impressive loyalty of a public who have had only their occasional ups and more than their fair share of downs over the years. City had escaped from the tightest corner in their history.

But even though things might have improved on the field in the second half of 1998-99, there has still been internal squabbling at boardroom level and a general uncertainty and lack of stability off the pitch. How much longer will they stay at Boothferry Park after the threats of having to go to Hull FC's Boulevard home for ground-sharing and the promise of a purpose-built multi-sport stadium in or around the city? Not surprisingly, the Tigers' fans generally oppose the former with some venom and remain wary of the ramifications and the likelihood of the latter. It is a healthy suspicion based on years of anti-climax and disappointment amid all the under-achievement. Top-flight soccer in Hull remains as far off as ever as the club's centenary gradually approaches. It should never, of course, have got to this sorry state of affairs in the first place, but Hull City fans remain gallantly resilient and their collective hopes spring eternal. If only…